Dear Santa

Dear Santa

Edited by
SAMUEL JOHNSON OAM

Illustrated by
SHAUN TAN

hachette
AUSTRALIA

⊡ hachette
AUSTRALIA

Published in Australia and New Zealand in 2018
by Hachette Australia
(an imprint of Hachette Australia Pty Limited)
Level 17, 207 Kent Street, Sydney NSW 2000
www.hachette.com.au

10 9 8 7 6 5 4 3 2 1

A catalogue record for this
book is available from the
National Library of Australia

NATIONAL
LIBRARY
OF AUSTRALIA

ISBN: 978 0 7336 4186 2 (paperback)

Cover and internal design by Christabella Designs
Cover and internal illustrations by Shaun Tan
Typeset in Garamond Regular by Kirby Jones
Printed and bound in Australia by McPherson's Printing Group

MIX
Paper from
responsible sources
FSC
www.fsc.org   FSC® C001695

The paper this book is printed on is certified against the
Forest Stewardship Council® Standards. McPherson's
Printing Group holds FSC® chain of custody certification
SA-COC-005379. FSC® promotes environmentally
responsible, socially beneficial and economically viable
management of the world's forests.

Contents

Brian Mannix 40

John Paul Young 42

Louise Munnoch 43

Ian 'Molly' Meldrum 45

Shaun Micallef 48

Jo Stanley 50

Peter Phelps 52

Felicity Urquhart 55

John Williamson 56

Lyn Bowtell 57

Julie Koh 58

Shannon Noll 61

Toby Truslove 62

Michala Banas 65

Favel Parrett 67

Toni Tapp Coutts 69

Sophie Green 70

Vince Contarino 72

Stuart Coupe 73

Mary Anne Butler 76

Kevin Bennett 80

Greg Champion 82

Graeme Connors 84

David Taylor 85

Graham 'Buzz' Bidstrup 87

Brent Parlane 89

Angela Thompson 91

Shaun Tan 93

Rebecca Belt 97

Paris Mitchell 99

A message from the editor

A letter to Santa holds a child's dearest, most longed-for wish, committed to paper after copious thought with careful handwriting that screams 'nice', sealed in an envelope and sent to the end of the world with ... *hope*: hope that the letter will make it; hope that it will be read by an elf who doesn't need specs; hope that the yearned-for present may be delivered by a reindeer who isn't in sick bay. Hope that not having a chimney is okay.

Grown-up wishes go un-wished, the letters never written. Until now!

I asked Australia's most notorious and best-loved notables to write to Santa as an adult, in the name of cancer vanquishment. *None* of them were paid for their work, so that more profits from the sale of this book can be spent on cancer research. Their goodwill epitomises the spirit of Christmas, and to each author, thank you. Truly.

Dear Santa is just for fun, but it is also to help fulfil my most longed-for wish ... a cure for cancer.

Samuel Johnson OAM

Dear Santa

This probably isn't the type of letter you usually receive, because rather than ask for a present this year, I'd like to give you a gift. You do such an amazing job of making sure everyone else is happy that I wanted to do something to make your life a little more joyful.

The problem is, I didn't know what to give you. It seems to me that if you live in the world's biggest toy factory, you can probably make yourself whatever you need. So I'm offering you a night off.

This Christmas, I've assembled a task force of mates to help deliver presents for you. Aaron will take care of Africa, Nathan is in charge of North America, Steph is doing South America, and Euan is all over Europe. (You may have noticed that I chose people whose first initials match the continent they are serving. It's the only way I could keep the whole thing in my head.)

Unfortunately, Asia and Australia also start with A, and I now can't remember which one is the domain of Alice and myself. In fact, I'm now unsure that Aaron has Africa after all. My point is, you can have a night off while I take care of it all. Maybe watch the Carols by Candlelight with Mrs Claus. Or is that a bit of a busman's holiday?

I just have one question: do you mind if I borrow the reindeer for the night? I promise to be careful, fly slowly and not dent them. I'll even have them cleaned before I return them. (I assume there's a drive-thru deer wash you use?)

Please let me know if all this sounds good to you, and I'll lock in Aaron, Nathan, Steph, Euan and Alice.

All the best, and if it's not too early to say this – Merry Christmas.

Adam x x x

Adam Hills: comedian, TV host and inventor of the drive-thru deer wash

Dear Santa

Look, frankly all I want is a sleep-in and a restful day, okay, but I know how this is going to roll: I'll be woken up at about 4.10 am by the children insisting they have to open their presents immediately; it'll be 37 degrees in Queensland by about 11 am and everyone's tempers will be fraying in the heat; and by about 4 pm, I'll hate myself for eating and drinking too much.

In lieu of the lie-in I could ask for world peace, but I figure somebody else will do that and the way things are in world politics at the moment, fat chance.

So instead, I'm going to ask for some huge things, and I know you're not God so these are big requests, but if you could do your best to deliver the following, I'd be much obliged:

My friend Julie has oesophageal cancer. She's only just retired, her husband Mick is pretty close to joining her and they just want a chance to enjoy some years together after working hard all their lives and raising four kids. If you could get her through this, that would be great.

Also, my friend Grace was diagnosed with Stage 3 breast cancer in her early twenties. She's had the all-clear now for a couple of years. Can we keep that going, please? Into late old age?

And since we're in this space now, why don't we just get rid of cancer full stop? Then, next year I can just ask for a Prada handbag with complete impunity.

Yours sincerely,

Leigh

Leigh Sales: Head of Accountability, ABC

Dear Santa

My name is Grant and I think you're cool. I like to race cars and reckon it's amazing you can get around the whole world in one night.

Do you ever have to use the toilet in my house when you bring presents? Because you can. As long as you put the toilet seat down because my mum comes to stay and she hates that.

I need to apologise. I'm sorry I hit my teacher in the head with a golf ball when I was in Year 9. I've never forgotten it and I'm worried you haven't either. I'm not a bad boy – I found the ball during an excursion to the park and I just threw it as far and as hard as I could to impress my friends. Turns out, I threw it in the same direction as my teacher Mr Heard. I didn't know I could throw a ball 150 metres. Unluckily for Mr Heard, turns out I can.

The ball went so high into the clouds then came down and hit him right on the head. It made quite a funny noise, although it was not funny for long. When he dropped to the ground, I ran straight up to him and admitted it was me, once he regained consciousness. I hope this shows you that I took responsibility for my actions. His six stitches healed up well and I didn't even get detention. So if it's okay, let's not talk about this again.

I don't need a present this year, but if it's possible, please bring some rain for our farmers. They grow food for all of Australia, so they're really important people. They need help because some can't even afford to feed themselves in this terrible drought. Everyone deserves to be able to afford to live and eat.

I have an idea! Maybe when you're flying in your sleigh you can throw a rope around a cloud and drag it over Australia to make it rain? They are called *rein*deer after all. (That was a joke.)

So, thanks for reading my letter, Santa. Don't tell Mum about the golf ball incident. Feel free to use my toilet, and thanks for being the best.

Your friend,

Grant

Grant Denyer: enthusiastic Gold-Logie-winning game show host

Dear Santa

For Christmas this year I don't want presents. It's 1983, I'm ten, and I'm too old now for that childish Santa business. I like pop stars like Madonna and Paul Young, and grown-up songs about sexy stuff like kissing. BUT, I'd still be stoked to get a Big M chocolate-flavoured hula hoop, or roller skates, or the new Kajagoogoo album this year, if you've got some spare.

Presents aside, I just want some truth from you, Santa. I'm deeply confused. Who are you, really? Why is it that you are the only stranger allowed into everyone's house while we're asleep? Seriously, if creepy Mr Marshall from across the road in Ash Court crawled down our chimney, Mum would call the cops, but somehow, because it's you, it's okay.

Mum doesn't even mind, even though I reckon you're a bit of a pig leaving all those half-chewed biscuits and carrots when you're done. And further to that, how do you even get in on Christmas night? We don't actually have a chimney. You'd think we'd hear you making a racket, especially considering all those empty beer bottles you leave behind that Dad says were for the thirsty reindeers.

I also saw someone on the TV who looked a lot like you. He had a lustrous grey beard, a twinkle in his eye and a warm singing voice with a country twang. He sang his song with a blonde woman who was round and skinny and pointy, all at the same time. They seemed very much in love. They sang about islands and streams and sailing away. I loved him, Santa. And then I realised why. He looked just like you.

Santa, my question for you is this: are you Kenny Rogers? Is that why Mum says when she sees Kenny on TV that he'd be welcome to sweep her hearth anytime, and Dad just looks annoyed and walks out to the shed and stays there for ages? So – although your face hasn't changed as much as Kenny's has over the years ... stay real, Santa!

Love,

Myf xx

Myf Warhurst: ABC Radio, Spicks and Specks *host, Eurovision, invented the lesser-known 'Warhurst' sausage*

Dear Santa

I KNEW you were real!

I remember bursting into tears when I was seven and Claudie McLeay tried to tell me behind the tuckshop that you didn't exist at all, and it was my parents who left the presents.

And then, some time later, I will never forget when I finally worked up the courage to ask Mum about it. I will always cherish her robust denials over what Claudie had said.

It wasn't just that she was so outraged at the very suggestion that you were made up, it was that by this time – and I am not making this up – I was already old enough to have been sent from the field against the All Blacks for violence.

That didn't matter to Mum.

What mattered was that the magic of Santa be preserved for me against all comers, and I have taken her word for it ever since.

So, go well, Santa.

We believe in you.

Fly. Work. Work your magic!

And Merry Christmas to you, too.

Peter

Peter FitzSimons: Rugby Union player turned journo, presenter and author, and Chair of the Australian Republic Movement

Dear Santa

I'm really sorry my dog bit you. Again. As I mentioned in my apology letter last year, her name is Bella and she's a rescue dog, and for reasons we don't completely understand she has some issues with men. And people wearing hats. And people with facial hair. Also, sunglasses. Basically, if you have anything on or around your face she will lose her shit.

It's not her fault. Since the unfortunate incident last year where you shed quite a lot of blood in and around the fireplace, presumably at the location of your entrance to deliver presents, we consulted with a dog trainer, or a 'whisperer', as everyone who knows anything about anything, or perhaps just downloaded a PDF from the internet, is now called. His name was Graham and he told us that we needed to stop making excuses for whatever past she may have had before coming to us, and that she was just being unreasonable with the biting. And that some dogs are just nuts. He believes she is one of those dogs.

I floated my theory with Graham that perhaps she just had highly attuned facial recognition software installed in her brain, and any perceived alteration to the facial area in the form of hats, sunglasses, facial hair or a new fringe caused the software to malfunction to the point where she no longer recognised the face and decided to bite whatever body part was closest to the ground. Graham said that was bullshit. So anyway.

Once again, please accept my sincere apologies and I do hope that the delicious quinoa muffins (gf) that I left out for you to snack on helped to dull the pain. On the bright side, your suit is great camouflage for blood. So there's that. And it was a great strategy to leave the reindeer on the roof because last week Bella ate a possum.

All the very best, and this year we will for sure try to remember to tie Bella up far away from the Christmas tree.

Mia xxxx

Mia Freedman: founder of Mamamia, media whoopsy

Dear Santa

Thanks again for allowing me to reach out to you by mail. I sincerely appreciate how old-school you are with your communications. I can't begin to tell you how frustrating it can be trying to hear back from the Easter Bunny through his Facebook page. No matter how many likes I give him.

Anyway, I just wanted to let you know how much I appreciate what you do. Since I was little you have always remembered to bring me something every Christmas. (That giant Superman doll you got me when I was six was incredible. He even talked!) Even when I had a little one of my own asking for things too, you never forgot about me. (That giant Batman doll you got me last year was incredible. He even talked!)

I was thinking about it all recently and it made me realise something: you dress in a red suit, fly at top speed around the world, and make sure every kid and even grown-ups are happy on Christmas Day. I guess what I'm saying is, to me, you are the real superhero.

Now, up, up and away. You've got deliveries to make.

Love,

Rove

PS If you don't mind passing on my friend request to the Tooth Fairy, I'd greatly appreciate it.

Rove McManus: triple Gold Logie winner (greedy), whose real name is John

Dear Santa

Do you think you could unclusterf**k this situation I'm in right now?

If not, I'll settle for a tabletop arcade game.

Thanks in advance,

Deb

Deborah Mailman: actor and Australian gem

Dear Santa

What I want this Christmas is very simple. So simple, in fact, that if you could see my face right now I think you'd guess what it is straight away. The grey, hollow rings. The forgotten-about hair. Last week's eyeliner still haunting my cheeks. A little bit of something mysterious (food? baby vomit?) encrusted on my earlobe.

It's something I *used* to have in abundance. God, that's the arrogance of youth, isn't it: we never know how bloody grateful we should be at the time. We spend all those years complaining about chores, homework, love-life … the drama and the trauma and the ecstasy! Tumbling over and over on repeat inside our self-obsessed, sleep-drenched, maple-syrup minds.

And we take it *all* without thought. We steal it from our parents! We steal it from the weekend because we *know* that we can get it back whenever we want. We take it any which way we can, dear Santa, because we damn well can.

Now I have a toddler and a three-week-old baby. The baby won't sleep unless she's on me. Like, literally lying on top of me. My skin must be radiating some kind of heroin-like drug because she'll fall asleep straight away like this. I put her down in the cot on her back and PING! She'll open her eyes and start grunting like a constipated piglet or just outright wailing. If there's anywhere or any position I could put her in that might allow me some sleep, it's a no-go situation for her. Basically, Santa, she's not happy unless I'm wide awake, deliriously fantasising about my pre-baby twenties and holding back tears while trying not to tweet about it.

Even four hours in a row right now would be heaven! Oh! Absolute heaven! I shudder to think what I could achieve during the day with that much. I could write a book! Record a triple album! Become the new female Elon Musk and send some shit into space just because I can! Or maybe, just maybe, I could get out of my pyjamas and wash my hair.

Look it's simple, Santy (can I call you that?), it won't take much of your time. Just pause the present-throwing and weird chimney-creeping for a night and come on over here. Knock on the door like a normal bloke. I'll heat you up some milk – no, it's not for you – we can put it in the baby bottle and for God's sake you can do the night shift. Are we clear? All I want for Christmas, Santa Claus, is a little fucking sleep.

Yours,

Missy

Missy Higgins: nine-time Aria winner

Dear Santa

Can we just talk this year?

I've been pretty spoilt over my 29 years as a patron of Christmas. Mad respect for all the socks, chocolate and toys. And big thanks for the year you got us a trampoline – Uncle John breaking his ankle doing a backwards-triple-flip-unplanned dismount was definitely a gift that kept on giving.

But this year, I was wondering if you can do me a favour. I don't get presents anymore, so this one isn't for me, it's for the other young humans out there. This year, when you deliver presents can you also drop off a dash of confidence for everyone?

'Cos we all know you've got plenty to spare! You wear fire-engine red all season long – you don't give a shit about fashion. You are beloved for your bulging belly; no fat shaming ever happened in your world. You deliver presents to millions of kids across the globe in a single night and never have an ounce of self-doubt that you can manage the task (even as the population rapidly expands).

The kids out there could use a little of your self-esteem. Just sprinkle it on their candy (and yes, I'm aware spiking lollies sounds like a super-dodgy situation).

But I'm serious. I think it's the most useful gift you can give them.

Self-esteem empowers and encourages. It drives and defines. It makes a young person capable and happy and productive and keen. It gives them the confidence to try and not be so hard on themselves if they fail. It makes them kinder to themselves (and others).

So, this Christmas, Santa-Oh-Buddy-Oh-Pal, drop off a bit of self-assurance to the young ones. Oh, and don't let what I said about the colour red affect your style. You do you, buddy.

Cheers,

Amy

Amy Hetherington: terminally positive comedian and writer

Dear Santa

We were talking over some things here in faux-Bohemia the other night. The trees have disrobed their leaves and that ol' flirty sun is making coquettish moves into every corner, teasing us all. The seasons are cleaving; it's time to take stock.

We were discussing the possibility of dividing up the folks we know into those who would rather buy an economy-class ticket to Hades rather than ask another human to do them a favour, and those who don't give it a second or third thought. I consider myself one of the former, so I'm not going to ask for something and not proffer something in return, at the very least.

You get ramrodded with requests regularly. It's only going to get busier for y'all, but you may notice on your ledgers that I haven't asked for anything present-like for 40 years. Not bad, huh?

All I ask is for you to keep an eye on my girl in the season where your powers must be at their greatest. It's gonna be cold in NYC. I simply ask that she's warm. From all historical depictions of you, I can sense an awareness of sartorial commonsense. (And bugger those who criticise your perennial trust in reds, whites and blacks. Dress to suit yer cheeks, I say! All four of 'em.)

In return for what I ask, I will continue to smile at strangers, and try to ease off the ol' habitual. Again, if I am to base my impressions of you on the historical characterisations, we probably share a love of Aunty Ethanol, but I'll try to hold off until I can shout you one or two, and be grateful for the luck of a semblance of health.

Could you keep an eye on her, please?

I sure do appreciate your time, Sir.

The sky is beginning to bruise. See you out there.

TR

Tim Rogers: indie rock god

Dear Santa

My last letter to you was around 27 years ago, I think, asking for a pair of rollerblades. You never let me down, Santa. There they were, waiting for me at the bottom of the stairs. Purple and green perfection.

How were you to know that I lived on a hill and would careen down it on those blades Christmas morning 1991 and rip skin off every limb on my gangly body? I don't blame you at all, though. I want to clear that up right off the bat.

Santa, the thing is, life has sped up a lot since then. The Christmas spirit doesn't have time to kick in as hard when you're not at school making decorations for the classroom on December 1st, singing Christmas carols, watching Christmas movies instead of learning maths, writing Christmas cards for your whole grade and walking out of school on December 23rd knowing you don't have to return for six whole weeks. When you grow up, you careen towards Christmas like me going down that hill on rollerblades, frantically buying presents, working, working, working, trying to fit in as many catch-ups as you can before December 25 because everyone 'wants to get together before Christmas'. It makes me anxious, Santa. I used to look forward to it so desperately. Now … it sort of scares me.

So, this year, I ask you to use your magic and send to my stocking some of the joy and excitement that I had for Christmas in 1991. No more fear of it all ending in a bloody, gravelly mess at the bottom of the hill, but just flying with the wind in my hair, grin on my face and wonder in my heart. Is that too much to ask, Santa? Not for you, I know. You can do anything.

Christie

Christie Whelan Browne: doyen of musical theatre, #metoo champion

Dear Santa

Please please,
if you can,
if it's possible:

A giant-giant bed,
4 × 4 × 4 poster – at least,
one thousand softest-soft pillows,
silk-golden goose-down covers,
gold pink-purple sunset silk,
smooth-soothe satin silk.

An oval room –
giant oval room,
shaman smudged,
peonies blooming,
tuber roses,
spring jasmine climbing the 4 × 4 × 4 (at least),

a natural spring in a corner babbles,
fresh-pure water for all to drink.

One thousand slipper-sets,
Midnight-silk pyjamas and robes
Await.

The leaders of the world – all of them – arrive,
change into silks,
and together lie in the jasmine honey-silk soft
at dusk,
lie together – for sleep,
like kings of old.

Before sleep,
together,
tooth floss-brushing,
considerations of which side of the $4 \times 4 \times 4$
but it doesn't matter as the giant-giant poster bed is round,
no corners or angles to negotiate–navigate.

Then,
intimacies,
pillow talk,
other intimacies –
between
one,
some,
all,
before sleep.

This is sleep, spooning-sleep,
leaders of the world –
arms away,
tucked in around each other,
kitten-knotted,
sleep-talk-murmurs, purr-snores,
furry doona-muffled farts,
the leaders of the world –
all of them lie –
arms down – together.

Then Santa,
Bring the leaders of the world a dream
as they lie in this sweet-soft oval room
together
in the giant-giant poster bed,
a dream-vision of peace,
one that elevates these leaders of the world
above themselves.

As they lie,
intimate-spooning,
sleep breath-breathing
may they float, Santa,
fly-float
above, about, bigger than themselves,
in a float-dream of a quiet, shared, equal world
where everyone matters,
but no one more than another.

When they wake
rested, refreshed, changed,
without words,
with a knowing
of intimacy,
of humanity,
as they pull on socks and jocks and skirts and pants,
picking sleep from their eyes,
yawning.

They depart elevated,
bigger than they were,
armed with a dream,
shared,
of a quiet, equal world.

Penelope

Penelope Bartlau: creative performance maker, regular host of community Biscuit Readings

Dear Santa

I know it's only August, but the trees are up in DJs, and there are only 133 shopping days until Xmas ... so I thought I'd get in early. (I say 'shopping days', but in fact there are 133 'normal' days until Xmas, as you can shop on any of these days. I think it's just an old turn of phrase. Is that the case in Lapland, too? I remember when you couldn't shop on a Sunday, in which case those 133 days would have been 114 shopping days. And that's before even factoring in half-day closing on Wednesdays, which I remember as well – I'm sure you do, too, being very old and all that.)

Anyway, I wanted to make sure my letter is near the top of the pile. I'm assuming you have a system for letters. Like at the Medical Centre, perhaps, where they slip new forms under the older forms, to keep the queueing fair. (Having said that, this might not always be a completely foolproof method, as I sometimes see people, who I'm sure have come in after me, see the doctor first – at which point I give the receptionist a look which is part concern and part disdain.

I may even get up, walk to the desk and cast my eye over the row of remaining forms and say something like, 'How many people are ahead of me? I've been here for quite some time ...' Then I feel a bit bad – those receptionists work hard enough as it is and are doing the best job they can. I overcompensate later with a massive 'thank you' when my name is called, and offer a warm smile.)

Look, whatever works for you. You've obviously been doing this a long time. Perhaps you even have administrative help? Or Mrs Claus does some clerical work for you? Do the elves help with the letters, or are they just making old-fashioned wooden toys in the workshop?

But please don't tell me you just pile the letters up and mine will be at the bottom. Although that would actually work for me if you have a big opening session nearer to Xmas, as mine would end up near the top of the pile again as you cast aside envelopes and place the actual letters on top of each other ...

Oh, and all I want is socks. No, really! A selection of those Happy Socks. Something funky, but not too cartoony and childish. I want people to think I have an edge when they catch a glimpse above my brogues as I cross my legs, but I don't want them to think I'm trying too hard. Maybe a bright geometric pattern or stripes; spots are borderline. But definitely NO hearts, pineapples or leopard prints.

Maybe I'm overthinking this; I have a tendency to do that, Santa ...

Rob

Rob Pegley: writer, producer, SBS

Dear Santa

All I want for Christmas is the gift of appreciation.
It's that simple – and that hard.

Love – and thanks,

Luke

PS Could you please make it highly contagious!?

Luke O'Shea: Golden Guitar winner

Dear Santa

I don't want much, thanks, just a packet of lollies. My friend gave me some in America, but I've forgotten their name. They're small pellets of liquorice with different-coloured sugar coatings, but there's a little taste of aniseed in there, too, and I can't stop thinking about them. Thanks, Santa, I hope you can scan the world and find the ones I mean.

All the very best,

Helen

Helen Garner: icon, writer

Dear Santa

For many years I have scoured name mugs in hundreds of shops. Every time, I carefully check each name from Aaron to Zoe in case a hungover shop assistant has had a lapse in concentration and put the 'Hildegaard' mug in between, say, Phillip and Phyllis.

Alas, the shop assistants have an impeccable track record when it comes to placing things in alphabetical order. Perhaps these assistants should receive an extra bonbon in their stocking this time around.

This is the year.

A mug with 'Hildegaard' wrapped around it in a bright, strong, solid sans serif font would be much appreciated, and loved for many years to come – preferably each letter in a different colour.

Thanks in advance,

Hildegaard

PS A twelve-month period without another member of my dwindling family dying would also be appreciated, should the degree of difficulty of the above request prove too much.

PPS Please don't see this offer of a B option as an easy way out. I want that mug.

Hildegaard Hinton: prison officer, author

Dear Santa

This is a letter of objection. I'm not complaining, because I'm sure you mean well, but you are clearly responsible for several questionable business decisions that, like it or not, have been adopted by humans to rather deleterious effect. Let me explain, and I know you're busy trying hard, so I won't mince my words.

Firstly, you are fat. Since you started giving people what they want, they have also become fat. Coincidence? I suggest not.

You also teach that if we behave well for others, we will get what we want as a reward. You've turned virtue into a door prize. People expect a return on goodness now, which is quite sad to say the least. That's on you.

You have provided haven for paedophiles everywhere. They hide behind your beard and your belly and normalise kids sitting on strangers' laps. Ew.

You endanger deformed reindeer whose noses clearly need looking after. Their bulbous noses are proof of mistreatment, clearly, and it's disgusting.

Your factory model, which of course relies on the enslavement of minors, has been mirrored by our multinationals here. I thought you were on the same side as the kids?

Don't even get me started on your carols. Or the promiscuity under the mistletoe you openly promote.

Don't get me wrong, Santa. You didn't make us fat, expectant, damaged, spoilt, materialistic twits. But you certainly didn't help.

I hope you meet with a bloody partridge in a pear tree one day and I can see how you fucking like it. No no no. Not a merry Christmas. I'd rather accelerate myself into the holiday road toll than keep up with your piss-weak antics. Go fuck yourself.

From a very naughty boy ... because of you, probably.

Sam

Samuel Johnson: retired de-lebrity, long-distance unicyclist, Head of Cancer Vanquishment at Love Your Sister, co-editor of The Stick

Dear Santa

Jan Fran here. I'm the chick who hosts *The Feed* on SBS VICELAND. You watch SBS VICELAND, don't you? Thought so! But I wouldn't blame you if you didn't, tbh. I've been hosting *The Feed* for three years and my grandmother still thinks it's a food show. She's a real idiot.

Anyway, look, I won't take up too much of your time, 'cos I know you're busy breaking into people's houses 'n' all, but I do have one wish this Christmas. I was wondering if you might help get refugee kids off Nauru.

See, Nauru is this tiny island in the Pacific Ocean where we send some of the world's most vulnerable people, including children. Some of the children have known no other life than one lived behind a wire fence. Others are in a catatonic state – they don't eat, they don't sleep, they don't move – because of the trauma that comes from languishing in this island prison indefinitely.

I know, I know, it's not a very easy wish to grant – heck, there are folks in Australia who've been trying to get kids off Nauru for years – but our parliament just won't listen. Keeping folks in detention on the island is about the only thing our major parties agree on.

You might be the only one who can fix it, Santa.

Love,

Jan Fran

PS Sorry to get political at Christmas, I can't help it. I'm a real hoot at Christmas lunch after a few chardys, trust me.

Jan Fran: writer/producer/presenter who speaks three languages, most of them terribly

Dear Santa

They say the greatest trick the devil ever pulled was convincing the world he doesn't exist. Well, it seems you pulled off that trick quite nicely yourself. Notwithstanding mild concerns about the anagrams of Santa/Satan, I think you can use those powers for immense good.

I'm writing to propose you join the CIA as an in-field operative, gathering crucial anti-terror intelligence. Your incredible skill at home invasion, your expertise at crossing borders undetected and your ability to speak multiple languages make you the ideal undercover agent. Throw in the fact that most people don't even think you're real, and we have the makings of a perfect government spook.

I understand you may have some objections to this offer, such as the fact that you aren't particularly popular in Muslim countries where we, perhaps unfairly, focus our anti-terror efforts. You might also bring up the fact that as a citizen of the North Pole you have no allegiance to the USA. But, we consider ourselves world citizens, as I'm sure you do. And, since everyone likes getting presents no matter what religion, we think you'd be welcome pretty much anywhere (if you're spotted at all).

All we ask is for you to log any suspicious activity within 'hot zones', implant bugs into some known targets' homes, and ensure Vladimir Putin remains on the naughty list. In return, we will gift you with a brand-new Tesla sleigh designed by Elon Musk, complete with GPS, stealth technology and a next-generation SONOS sound system.

If you give us only one thing for Christmas this year, please let it be this.

Yours sincerely,

Sergeant Tim Hawken

Project Lead – Operation Secret Santa

Tim (TS) Hawken: writer, known for enjoying romantic midnight strolls to the beer fridge

Dear Santa

It has come to my attention that once again I am on the list of naughty people rather than the list of nice people. Who the hell gave you the right to determine such matters? What idiot made you judge, jury and executioner? It must be lovely to look down your nose and judge people you don't even know. Where do you get off? The North Pole!

The allegations against my character are bullshit and you know it. Just to clear things up – Barnaby Joyce got the girl pregnant, not me. Furthermore, I have never met Harvey Weinstein and certainly never attended one of his parties. Also, I have never said Kim Jong-un is a fun guy or encouraged Julie Bishop to take up pole dancing. These charges are simply not true.

As are allegations that I helped write Paul McCartney's song 'Fuh You'. I actually told Paul it was a shit lyric and that he was too old to be singing about sex.

I am not, nor have I ever been, on the coaching staff at the

Carlton Football Club. They are shithouse all by themselves and need no help from me!

Furthermore, I think it's a bit rich that you lob into town once a year and make these accusations with little to no proof.

I also think you should have a good hard look at yourself in the mirror. Firstly, you dress like a can of coke. Your beard and hair are unkempt. You are morbidly obese. What kind of message is your fatness sending to our children? You are supposed to be a role model, yet you seem more interested in encouraging children you don't even know to sit on your knee.

Quite frankly, you make me sick. I never have any problems with the Easter Bunny and I have a great relationship with the Tooth Fairy. The problem here is not me, it's you! So, stop being bloody-minded and get on with the job of handing out presents, you fat fool.

I'll expect a million dollars and a letter of apology in my stocking.

Cheers,

Brian

PS How much are you paying those elves in your North Pole sweatshop?

PPS I know a lot of people leave a beer out for you, but could you drink responsibly this year? Waking up on Christmas morning to find several pools of your vomit on the floor is not ideal, and if your reindeer take a shit, pick it up!

Brian Mannix: Winner of Mr Ocean Grove, 1971

Dear Santa

My name is John Paul Young and I really have been behaving myself for a long time now, a lot longer than the twenty or so years I have been waiting for my state government to clean up my local creek that THEY made a mess of in the '70s and '80s through mining. Can you please ask them to do something about it?

Also, could you please give our politicians a boost of courage so that they can fix the mess they have made of our transport and infrastructure.

And last but not least, could you please, please give a big dose of empathy to those in our society who refuse to display such a quality to those less fortunate than themselves. That would be good for us all.

Wishing you a Merry Christmas and safe travels.

John

John Paul Young: Countdown *megastar, ARIA Hall of Fame inductee*

Dear Santa

Well, I had all these great ideas about asking for world peace, pay equality and the resignation of President Cheezel, but things have got a bit desperate in our house, so I've had to change the plan.

This year I'd like you to bring me five more years to enjoy my daughters, despite what the oncologist said. If possible, I'd also like some research boffin somewhere to ignore the fact that I'm ineligible for all the new immunotherapy trials and sneak me in – I promise I will do my damnedest to make their numbers look awesome.

And if you can't bring me either of these, I guess then I need you to bring me a bucketload of acceptance with a side of resignation. Neither of these have been in large supply around here lately.

And maybe my girls could use a layer of toughness, because they've been crying a lot lately when they think I don't hear.

Regards,

Not Dead Yet in Gosford

PS If you can't bring me any of these things, please make sure your sleigh and reindeer land firmly on top of You-Know-Who, since he/she is such a dickhead. Dying has not made me noble.

Louise Munnoch: patient advocate at Love Your Sister, writer for The Stick

Dear Santa

You've always been pretty good to me. Every year you deliver the Boxing Day Test, which, for a cricket tragic like me, is a wonderful gift. You also bring lots of great music and treats for Ziggy.

I wish you were able to make the world the place that John Lennon imagined in 'Imagine'. No greed, no hunger, with everyone equal, sharing the world and making it a better place. That's my dream.

Selfishly, can I also ask for something for myself? I appreciate everything you do, Santa, especially as you know that I haven't always been a good boy. I play my records too loud, and every now and then I have a party that might annoy the neighbours.

But I promise, Santa, that I'll stop being naughty if you give me the one thing I crave most:

A St Kilda premiership.

Surely I'm not asking for too much, Santa?

I was hoping it was going to be this year. The St Kilda

president said we had a team capable of finishing in the Top Four. Instead, we won just four games and finished sixteenth.

I've been blessed with Logies, gold records and ARIA Awards. But St Kilda's trophy cabinet contains just one premiership cup. It's lonely, Santa. It needs a mate.

Yes, Santa, I admit again that I'm occasionally a naughty boy. But please don't bring me any more wooden spoons. We already have enough of those – more than any other club.

As you know, St Kilda were a founding member of the VFL in 1897. In fact, before joining the VFL, the Saints were a foundation club of the VFA in 1877. We never won a VFA premiership, so that means that in 141 years we have had just one successful season.

Just one.

Sure, we've gone close a few times. In the 1971 Grand Final we led Hawthorn by 20 points at three-quarter time. But the Hawks kicked seven goals in the last quarter and won by seven points. That was Hawthorn's second premiership. Since then, they've won another eleven flags, while we didn't appear in another Grand Final for 26 years. That year, 1997, we finished on top of the ladder. On Grand Final day we played the Adelaide Crows, who finished fourth. They kicked eight goals in the last quarter to beat us by 31 points. It was Adelaide's first premiership. They'd been in the competition for seven years; we'd been there for 100 years.

The Crows won their second flag a year later. Is that fair, Santa?

I'm not the most religious man, but surely you should reward saints more than sinners? Yet, the Saints have won just one flag, while the Melbourne Demons have won twelve.

You're a saint yourself, Santa, so I can't understand why you've treated your fellow saints so poorly.

Of course, I was there in 1966 when the Saints played Collingwood in the Grand Final. In fact, I was a proud member of the cheer squad. At the 27½-minute mark of the last quarter, the scores were tied. Then eighteen-year-old Barry Breen grabbed the ball and kicked at the goals. It wobbled through for a behind. St Kilda was in front!

The crowd went up … and I went down. The drama and the tension were too much for me. I fainted. As the siren sounded, I was down for the count. So, Santa, I've never actually seen St Kilda win a Grand Final.

I was there again in 2010 when, if not for a bad bounce, we might have beaten Eddie's Magpies. The previous year, we might have beaten the Cats – if not for Matthew Scarlett's famous 'toe poke'.

If, if, if … yes, I know that's a lot of ifs, Santa. But if you can deliver the Saints just one more flag, I'll be a good boy.

I promise.

Molly

Ian 'Molly' Meldrum: the bloke with the hat, the ladder and the mumbles

Dear Santa

I write with a heavy heart, for the only thing I ask from you this festive season is for you to take me off your Xmas List.

It's not the fact that you insist on being called Santa – which is way too Norman-Rockwell-Coca-Cola American for me – it's that I've just realised you are a dumbed-down version of God. Admit it: you have a big white beard, you can defy the laws of space and time, you can watch everybody in the world all at once, and you reward goodness (with presents/Heaven) and punish badness (with coal – which is burned, as it would be in the fires of Hell).

I guess it's okay for kids to believe in you. That's kind of sweet. And I suppose it's nice that once a year we can all view humanity through the eyes of our children and pretend that goodwill and fellowship still exist. Because belief is a type of pretending, isn't it – and if we all pretend hard enough, then goodwill and fellowship will exist as a sort of mass consciousness. And from that will spring Hope and Love. And then Peace on Earth.

Mind you, if I'm honest, these good feelings are not so much down to you as repeated screenings of *It's a Wonderful Life* over the holidays.

You are and will remain a mass-produced shill for capitalism.

And I remain your faithful servant,

Shaun

PS God Bless Us One and All.

Shaun Micallef: certifiable genius

Dear Santa

(or whoever you are),

It's done. My kid has worked out you are a fraud, and I'm so happy.

I grew up fully aware you weren't real. I always knew the Tim Tams we left out on Christmas Eve were for our mum. It was a fun game that meant no lies were told, but she still got to binge on chocolate biscuits. Good on her.

But when our baby came along, my husband insisted we 'keep the magic alive'.

Magic? Do you mean, 'He sees you when you're sleeping, he knows when you're awake'? Hey Santa, back off – you're a creep!

Or the threat that if you shout, cry or pout you get zip on Christmas morning? That's not magic, that's manipulation.

A truly magical childhood is being loved unconditionally and knowing that the gifts you receive on Christmas Day are because of that love. And do you know what else is magic? The power of gratitude.

I'm not anti-fantasy. Every childhood should be full of make-believe and the impossible – whether it's a dragon's lair made from an old sheet, a secret hide-out under a shrub in the garden, or slime making sense. None of that comes with rules made by adults.

But because it mattered to my husband, I tried to maintain the myth. Even though I hated it, and was very bad at it. I never used different wrapping paper for Santa presents. We never posted letters to the North Pole. And I could never look my daughter in the eye and lie. Any questions, I'd suddenly plunge headfirst into the depths of my handbag or find the back of my pantry fascinating, while mumbling something like, 'Daddy knows ...'

Thankfully, my kid is clever and I'm lazy. It took only a dinosaur shower cap, bought as a stocking filler and seen at our local chemist, and the whole system crumbled. She put two and two together, and I sang like a canary. I put the Easter Bunny and the Tooth Fairy under the bus, too. Best Christmas ever.

So I'm sorry, Santa, this is the first – and last – letter you'll receive from our household. And if you're wondering, I like it here on the Naughty List. We get all the Tim Tams.

Love,

Jo

Jo Stanley: broadcaster, children's author, warrior for hope

Dear Santa

Knowing this is peak time for you, Mrs Claus and the elves leading up to The Big Trip, sleighing it round the world with Rudolph and the mob, I appreciate your time in reading this and would love it if you could consider my request.

I have been fortunate enough to have seen a lot of the world and to learn from other cultures. This was mostly as a single, white male actor/writer/curious traveller who, much of the time, had travel, accommodation and meals paid for by the company that had hired me. I probably didn't fully appreciate this privilege at the time. I sure do now. And so a round-the-world trip is what I wish for my family this Christmas.

Now that I am the suburban dad in an urban artistic drought, I would like for me and my girls – my partner-in-life and teen and tween daughters – to have an experience like no one has ever had before. Except you, of course, Mr Claus. And that is where you come into it.

I need your help to deliver the best family Christmas present and the greatest adventure ever. There are a couple of ways it could be done, but here is what I reckon. We could go off our family 'nanas discovering four round-the-world flight tickets, guidebooks and spending money in four stockings hanging on our mantelpiece (I'll build one) on Chrissie morning; or you could lend us a spare sleigh (I'm sure you have one in the Claus family barn). My daughters, being junior animal activists, could look after your reindeer; we could see your wonderful work distributing good tidings, joy and gifts to every child in the world. But only the Christian ones, of course. We wouldn't impose Christmas on anyone who didn't want it. We'd learn from their cultures as we visited them. And maybe leave a 'thank you' gift, instead. (Oh, just a question, if you have nine reindeer for yourself, would that mean we'd need 36 reindeer pulling our family of four's sleigh?)

My family would also love to be a part of the freedom that must be a huge part of what makes you so jovial. We would love to join the only person to be allowed entry into every country in the world in a foreign vessel with no passport or visa and who never has to have animals quarantined. It must have been particularly difficult to continually gain entry over my own country's borders. You must have had some sort of arrangement with our government. I think that might be because you are flying everywhere and not coming by boat.

Of course, ever since you first came to our shores you've gone above and beyond, handing out goodies in the bush from utes and from rubber duckies in the surf, arriving by parachute and from underwater onto our beaches (damn you're good!), and you have never failed, sir. Well, except once.

(Even though I never got the bike I always wanted, I must thank you for coming through every year with the fort and cowboys and Indians set up on my bedroom floor, and the bulging pillowcase at the end of my bed full of everything I asked you for on your lap at Warringah Mall. How did you not catch my dad as he snuck out of my room after pulling off the string attached to my finger and the door knob?)

So, if you deliver on my Christmas request you would make my family's holiday/life. And, because you know EVERYONE, I'd like you to consider being executive producer of the doco we could make of the trip. I'd direct.

One last Chrissie wish just for me: If I send you the dimensions, a new surfboard. I've already got a travel cover and soft roof racks for the spare sleigh and/or reindeer.

Thanks heaps, Santa, and look forward to seeing you.

Peter

PS I hope you don't mind, but I asked Siri how old you are. First she said, 'I hear you get on the naughty list for asking that', then she said, 'Older than the winds of time and younger than a spring chicken'. You must have noticed how Siri can sometimes get all poet-y – on a third go she said, 'Roughly 1748 years. Give or take a century.'

You have visited every country in the world with the knowledge of every boy's and every girl's wants and needs and you know who's been naughty and who's been nice. That takes some sort of brain-teaser mind power; 1748 years old – I must get some tips for the Alzheimer's and dementia organisations as to how you do it.

Peter Phelps: much-loved TV legend, author

Dear Santa

I know how busy you are ... but I only have a small list this year.

1. I would like my internet to work. I understand world peace might be easier to achieve, but any improvement would be appreciated.

2. I would like my kids to listen and not ignore me when I'm calling the shots, especially when I threaten that they might make your naughty list!

3. Wine and chocolate.

Thanking you in advance,

Felicity

PS I'm in a small country town, in a house without a chimney, so please use the side entry.

Felicity Urquhart: singer, songwriter, broadcaster

Dear Santa

I don't want anything for myself, thank you. I would ask you, however, to pick up as many kids as you can and fly them over to Uluru in your sleigh. I want all Aussie kids to experience the true spirit of our ancient land. It will give them a much broader view of what it is to be Australian and perhaps help them understand the attachment our Indigenous people have with the earth instead of high-rise buildings.

John

John Williamson AM: Aussie music legend, ARIA Hall of Fame inductee

Dear Santa

Thanks for the bright-yellow Barbie bus you gave me in 1984. I think it's still getting around in one of my nieces' bedrooms. It's so tough, I'm pretty sure that it will never break down in landfill. Luckily it's being repurposed – Mattel built those plastic accessories to last!

I don't need anything in particular this year, but some better leaders in government wouldn't go astray – perhaps you could lend a few of your elves? Oh, and I'm still hoping for that Gold Record I requested when I was twelve.

Lots of love and Merry Christmas.

Lyn

Lyn Bowtell: alternative singer–songwriter, 2017 Team George (The Voice)

From: results@burnoutquiz.com
To: santasotheremail@gmail.com
Date: 25 Nov 2018, 03:39
Subject: Am I Experiencing Christmas Burnout?
[Your CONFIDENTIAL Test Results]

Dear K K,

Thank you for completing the online automated test 'Am I Experiencing Christmas Burnout?'. Your score fell within the 46–57 range, indicating a **Dangerous Level of Burnout**. This demonstrates that you are experiencing **significantly higher than average levels** of inefficiency, exhaustion and even cynicism. As the silly season approaches, know that you are not alone. Many people are likely to be feeling low from the effects of overwork and accumulated stress.

Your test results show that factors contributing to your end-of-year slump may include the following:

1. You deliver. High achievers are likely to find themselves in positions of leadership. Your perfectionism and ability to deliver may mean that people have come to rely on you to produce virtually magical results. You may attract endless, and sometimes impossible, requests from others, leading to severe fatigue.

2. You give too much. You have a habit of overgiving and even trying to buy the love of others. Folks might call you a saint, but your regular bouts of emotional spending are really just attempts to fill the emptiness inside. You exhibit co-dependent tendencies including people-pleasing. You constantly feel used and underappreciated. Do you find yourself giving to the same takers but never getting anything back? Have you developed abandonment issues from a succession of 'friends' deciding that they have outgrown you and no longer believe in you? Do you find that others wait for an appropriate moment to claim credit for your generous deeds?

3. You expect others to live up to your high standards. In your test responses, the words you used most frequently to describe others were 'naughty', 'nice' and 'hoe hoe hoe'. These are instances of extreme thinking, according to which you judge individuals as simply good or bad. In truth, people are generally many shades in between and cannot always meet your expectations. This does not make them undeserving. Remember: everyone is fighting their own battles. Your idealism, and resulting disappointment in the face of reality, may have led you to withdraw from regular society for significant periods of time. It can be lonely at the top.

4. You question your existence. You have indicated that you identify as male and are in the 100+ age group. At this stage in life, you are likely to have achieved major goals, and even some repute, but you may still feel unsatisfied. Perhaps your cheerful facade hides deep pain developed over years of adhering to an unrealistic personal myth. You may be in the midst of a psychological crisis so acute that you wonder if you even exist. Yet reaching out for assistance may be something you have tried to avoid, given that <u>men are less likely than women to seek professional help</u>.

But here's the good news, K K – all is not lost. By completing this online test, you have already taken your first step in the journey to recovery. For more information on how to deal with burnout and reach your full potential, **purchase my bestselling book, _The Subtle Life-Changing Magic Art of Not Giving._**

At this time of the year, I cannot emphasise enough the importance of self-care. If there is one wish that my team and I have this Christmas, it is that you make sure you take time off. Prioritise your wellbeing. Schedule that holiday. Put your feet up, and leave the astonishing feats of the season in the capable hands of good ol' Santa Claus.

Get rest, you merry gentleman!

Dr Julie Koh

Dr Julie Koh OAM
Life Coach | Acclaimed Author | Holistic Educationist

Dear Santa

Where do I start with my requests?

With my darling wife, three beautiful children and our fourth on the way, I feel like I already have it all. That said, I'll be selfish and ask you for two things anyway.

Please bring some love to our land in the form of rain. Give our farmers the gift of relief, as they are struggling more than ever before.

This leads to my second gift request: I'd like not just our farmers but everyone struggling to know they are not alone. Give all those who need it a hug and let them know they will be okay because we will stand by them.

These are big gifts to ask for, I know, Santa, but I think they are overdue and there is nothing else I want more at the moment, except maybe to come first one time in something … just joking!

Shannon

Shannon Noll: sheep shearer done good

Dear Santa

Important question: where will I address my letters when you move? I'm pretty sure it's been brought to your attention that chunks of the North Pole are breaking off and floating away. Apparently the whole place might be gone in a couple of years.

Have you noticed skinny polar bears and scared-looking seals drifting off on icebergs? I guess fairly soon the bit of the Pole that has your house (and the Santa factory with all the elves) will break off too. I'm sure the bears and seals will be fine – who doesn't like a summer holiday?

It's where *your* iceberg ends up that is more important to me. I mean, those presents aren't going to deliver themselves, right? To that end, I've got some suggestions on where to steer your iceberg (and Santa factory) when you break away from the Pole. Assuming you can steer the iceberg, could the elves whip up a rudder arrangement?

Anyway. You can head in one of two directions: through the Bering Strait towards the Pacific; or head into the Norwegian Sea towards the Atlantic. Both these directions have pros and cons.

I'm sure you're a bit touchy about man-made environmental fuck-ups at the moment, what with your country melting (sorry!), so I thought I'd highlight the ecological disasters in each direction so you can make an informed decision.

The Atlantic is very scenic, however you might want to avoid the Gulf of Mexico – the Deepwater Horizon incident was the biggest single oil-spill disaster in the world. But if you head to the Pacific side, avoid Prince William Sound, Alaska, where the *Exxon Valdez* crashed – it's still not great. To be fair, both those little spills pale in comparison to the ongoing catastrophe in the Niger River Delta where millions of gallons of oil have been spilt since oil exploration began there in the 1960s. But the iceberg would have trouble getting there, so don't worry about it.

The Pacific has a lot going for it. China would be a great spot to pull up the iceberg unless you're prickly about those carbon emissions. See, China's growth depends on coal providing 70 per cent of its energy – probably why it's the world's largest carbon emitter. (Fun fact for the elves: mining kills up to thirteen miners there every day.)

Also, there's the little problem of the raging underground coal fires that have burned in Inner Mongolia since the 1960s. On the other hand, the Pacific has the Great Pacific Garbage Patch. You'll probably see it as you float by. It's between California and Hawaii, and it's the world's largest garbage dump – a massive gumbo of plastic and rubbish reportedly three times the size of France floating in the ocean. Yeah, you'll definitely see it. I'm sure you'll chuckle to yourself when you think of all the disposable plastic toys that have contributed to it. Don't get stuck there, Santa! The irony!

Now, this is important. If you head the Atlantic way, remember to watch out for Bermuda. Not only might the Bermuda Triangle swallow your iceberg but, even worse, you'll be close to Haiti. That's a hotspot of disaster you'll want to avoid. Try the Dominican Republic, it's delightful. (Fun Q&A for the elves: Haiti and the Dominican Republic share an island and have similar geographic and climate conditions, so why do severe storms and hurricanes only cause horrific human tragedy on the Haitian side? Mostly it's due to the complete destruction of Haiti's trees by us humans!)

Finally, the Pacific will lead you to the east coast of Australia. I'd tell you to stop and look at the Great Barrier Reef, but we've pretty much cooked that, so I wouldn't bother. And to tell the truth, turning up in Australia on a damaged floating vessel trying to escape horror and hardship isn't a great idea. We tend to throw those seeking refuge onto prison islands. Maybe keep floating to the South Pole. I mean, it's melting something like three times faster than five years ago, but still, it'll be around a bit longer. I'm definitely sure we will have everything cleaned up by then. Definitely.

I'll send a copy of this letter to both the North and South poles just in case. And I'd like a Fitbit, or a scooter.

Love,

Toby

Toby Truslove: Aussie actor (Utopia)

Dear Santa

It has been a long time since I've written. Probably around 35 years, I reckon. Wow.

I believe the last time I wrote to you I was asking for two specific things I'd had my eye on and had been hassling my parents for. In my house, we were only ever allowed to ask you for one thing each year, but in my fourth year of life I was so torn by indecision, my parents let me ask you for an unprecedented TWO things. I lost my tiny mind when Christmas came, and I received BOTH of the items I had so desperately coveted – a pink ballet tutu and a plastic ride-on CHiPs motorbike. Just so you know, I wore that tutu while riding that motorbike. A lot. Like a boss.

Now that I'm a grown-up, it's interesting how much the things I wish and hope for have changed. The thing is, I don't want THINGS. I have things, and I am fairly fortunate in the fact that I don't really need or want very much these days. I really only wish for experiences and bravery and things you can't buy. Not even you can get them for me, Santa.

Or can you?

If a kid sits on your knee or writes you a letter and asks for the health of a loved one to be improved, or for more time to spend with their friend, or to have the courage to chase a dream, can you make that happen? Or are you limited to delivering on material presents only?

Hmmm.

So, since I don't need any THINGS, I suppose it's up to me to tackle the rest myself. I think I'm reasonably equipped to do that. I feel like I can be strong and delicate at the same time, and help to make a change in the world, even in a tiny way. There are some things I can't control, of course, but you probably can't control them either.

I guess this is really a thank you letter.

You helped a little girl to be more than just one thing. She now wears many hats and feels braver in the world each day.

So, thank you. Thanks for having an open mind and not judging my choices. You should know, I'm still the amazing ballet dancer and cool cop on the inside.

Michala

PS I know you are close with my mum and dad, so feel free to show them this letter. And give them both all my love.

Michala Banas: Australia's much-loved Upper Middle Bogan

Dear Santa

I have never written to you before, so I'm going to use all of my 44 years of Christmas wishes at once in the hope that you can help me. And I promise I've been good (well, mostly).

The only thing I want for Christmas is freedom for more than 100 refugee children who are imprisoned on Nauru. I want them to find safety. I want them to experience kindness. I want them to have the basic human rights all children deserve. Mainly, I want them to stay alive.

I know this is a lot to ask from one person, even if you are Santa. But then again, our prime minister is one person and he could get this done in the blink of an eye. So why doesn't he? Why didn't the prime minister before him do it? And the one before him?

Australia is wilfully damaging the health of children on Nauru to make a point – and I'm sure you find it as appalling as I do. It's a crime.

How many kids do you reckon you can fit in your sleigh?

Thank you in advance,

Your friend, Favel x

Favel Parrett: author, Miles Franklin Award shortlistee, bushwalker

Dear Santa

For Christmas I would like a TREATY to be signed for the healing and reconciliation of Australia in recognising the First Nations people and our true history, so that we can grow strong together and be proud as one nation.

Toni

Toni Tapp Coutts: Deputy Mayor who once trademarked graffiti on a railway bridge that read 'Jesus loves nachos' in the hope that it would boost tourism to the outback town of Katherine

Dear Santa

When I was little I believed in you. I'd leave carrots by the fireplace for your loyal Dasher, Dancer and friends. There may also have been some parental donations of brandy and biscuits.

I'd try to stay awake to hear your reindeers' hooves on the roof. One year I was sure I heard sleigh bells. Of course, on Christmas morning I'd rush to see what you left me. But the point of it, really, wasn't the presents – it was the magic of believing that something special happened on Christmas Eve.

There was one important person I shared that magic with: my brother, Nicholas, younger by two years. I'm not sure he was ever as invested in the whole thing as I was, but he was always keen to run to the tree in the morning to see what was there. And as I look back now, as a grown-up-type person, it is very clear to me that the magic of your myth, Santa, and the excitement of opening presents and everything else good that happens at Christmas, was more about him than anything.

My brother was the magic – the fun and excitement had more to do with him than anyone or anything else.

The Christmas presents 'from Santa' are long forgotten. What abides is the certainty that the greatest gift I've ever received was my baby brother. He's taller than me now, and we don't really have anything in common apart from memories. I like to chat; he's the strong, silent type. He likes team sports; I do not. But he's still magic, and over the years since our childhood an even greater gift has emerged: that of his friendship.

So, Santa, I'd like to say thank you for bringing some magic into our young lives and allowing me to see that the magic in my grown-up life comes from people, not things.

Merry Christmas,

Sophie

Sophie Green: Top Ten bestselling author who will holiday by the ocean in preference to anywhere else

Dear Santa

This year when you come to my house, can you please not clean up the reindeer poo? I want to put the poop on my tomatoes – apparently it's really good fertiliser and the tomatoes love it!

If you do that you can give my present to someone else, because reindeer poo is all I want for Christmas.

Love you, Santa. Bye!

Vince

Vince Contarino: Zep Boys frontman

Dear Santa

It's been a while. Trust you're keeping well. The last time we did this letter business I could barely write. Some say nothing much has changed, but it is actually what I do for a living. No more crayon scribbles for me, dude, I'm in the big league these days. You know, that ol' computer and typing stuff.

I'm not sure you're aware, but I was in the Santa Impersonator Business (SIB) for a while, getting down chimneys like you do so I could leave extra stuff for my kids – and I must admit from time to time I snacked out on the carrots and beer that they left for you and the 'deers. Kinda still feel bad about that.

Anyway, it's never too late to make a call on the big guy, right? When Christmas comes around, usually most of my non-Santa friends come good with stuff that I'm after, but this year I kinda need to call in the big one. No, not world peace, an end to climate change and another Sydney Swans premiership – but dude, keep working on all those as they're about the best gifts Santa could give the world; but you know that, don't you!

Okay, let's cut to the chase here, Santa. I'm pretty sure you've never been a big fan of the musical group the Grateful Dead. You may be, but I have no other way of explaining why my request for their second album was never fulfilled at your end back in the day. Okay, okay, maybe I was considered a little 'old' to be writing to you back then – but we're both over this ageism stuff, aren't we? So this year I'm looking to give you a redemption chance in the Grateful Dead stakes – but of course times have changed and the ask is just that bit bigger. As you may know, the Grateful Dead are one of my favourite rock'n'roll bands, but they release old concerts faster than you and your helpers can pack a stocking. Seriously, there are so many reissues and here's the thing – the new one, which, Santa, I REALLY REALLY WANT, is a nineteen-CD box set. This being 2018 I'm not going to describe it – here's a link; that's what all the down-with-it kids do these days:

http://www.dead.net/store/music/new-releases/pacific-northwest-73-74-complete-recordings-boxed-set

So that's what I'm after. Let me run through the essentials before I let you go. I've been really good all year. Really, really good. No social media outbursts. I kept calm when the Swans bowed out of the finals. I ate my greens and rang my mum every day. Cool with you? Okay – deal. Oh, and don't use the Santa Courier this year. They always rush off and leave one of those damn cards – 'Sorry I missed you – Santa'. Let's go back to the ol' chimney routine.

Still a VB guy? There'll be a case waiting. Oh, and the carrot – but screw that, I'll eat it. Least I can do. Give the reindeers a break with that side of things.

All the best, Santa.

Stuart

Aged 62

Stuart Coupe: broadcaster, band manager in another life (Hoodoo Gurus, Paul Kelly), author, music commentator

Dear Santa

I know I should be writing to you wishing for grown-up, selfless things like world peace, the removal of hunger and poverty, equality for all, no more wars or floods or cyclones, and no more cruelty or inequity.

But Santa is a kid's domain, and if I revert back to the selfish, centre-of-the-universe munchkin that I was when I still believed in you, I recall you gave me the microscope that I asked for *waaaaay* back in 1970.

Remember that, Santa? How I spent Christmas morning delirious with happiness, pricking everybody's fingers with a sewing pin, sluicing their pulsing blood onto my glass slides so that I could see all the tiny cells and platelets and plasma wriggle around under magnification. Pulling hairs out from visitors' heads to slip under the cover slip, thence to view their hollow, fractured differences under that bright investigative light. Man, that was the best present you ever brought me.

But clearly it's time to up the ante. Even though I should wish for equity for all, Santa, if I'm really, really, honestly true to the bottomless core of my bottomless soul, what I really, really want for Christmas is just to have my dad back again. For a bit. Just to see a tiny whisper of his deep-dimpled smile. Or, if there's enough room in your sleigh, then maybe some actual time with him. An hour? Would that be too much to ask?

It actually doesn't sound like much, written down all cold and hard like this. Is it too greedy to ask for a whole night of wining and dining and chit-chatting like we used to, into the wee hours until the sun once again rose? Or, if you're up for it, how does a whole day sound? Or a week? Or a month? Or a year? I mean, surely the effort lies in getting him here – once he's here it'll be just as hard to take him back again, so he might as well stay forever, right?

While I feel bad for not asking for my mum back right now – and as grateful as I am for all she did for me while still battling her own many-headed demons – truth be told, my dad and I had a different kind of bond, you know? A shared love of words. A shared love of books. A shared sense of humour. A shared love of wine. A shared sense of the absurd. We were cut from the same cloth, him and me. Not a jolly red Santa suit with happy white trimmings – ours was a far darker, heavier fabric: prone to thunder and impatience and the odd streak of judgement. But it was also multi-textured and layered, hard to pin down. Its collars were wrought from too many shades of complexity to settle into any useful form. Its colours changed daily depending on the light, or the wind. Its folds held large packs of growling black dogs, which nestled in to stay for the duration. But it was still the same cloth.

They say you can't miss what you didn't have – but I do, Santa. I do. I miss all the laughs we didn't laugh, all the chinwags we didn't chinwag, all the puns we didn't pun, all the wines we didn't wine, all the moments we didn't moment. He died when he was 69 and I was 36, and I still feel cheated by that. I feel thieved by time. And where the theft took place I have this aching, gaping, hurting longing for all the things we didn't do.

But even then, Santa, whatever amount of time I would have with him, knowing me as I do, I'd spend at least half of it upset and anxious, sure in the knowledge that while he would be here, right before me, he would only be here for a short time. Knowing I would surely lose him again, in the way of such losses. And my heart hurts even now, Santa, just thinking about losing him all over again. It aches, it really does. My heart aches and my chest hurts and my head throbs; and it's almost a thought too big for me to think. I don't think I could live through that, all over again.

So maybe I shouldn't ask for him back, after all. Maybe I should just raise a glass of wine up to the stars tonight – like I do some nights – wish my dad a fond farewell and recall in my heart all that we did do together, not what we didn't do. Maybe I should ask you instead for the wisdom to let the past be what it is: an aching, hollow, Dad-shaped space where the cold winds howl and still chill me to the core, at times. Maybe I should ask for the wisdom to put all the love and energy and hope of wishing him back alive straight into the living, breathing beings right before me – and let my dad just … be.

So actually, cancel that order, Santa. And then – with the space my dad doesn't take up in your sleigh – how's about you fill that with a bit of world peace, and the removal of hunger and poverty, and while you're at it make sure there's no more cruelty or inequity or wars or floods, and that there's enough equality for all. I hope you have a big sleigh this year, Santa. I think you're gonna need it.

But hey – and sorry to harp on – if there's still a smidgen of room after all that, if you could just slip in a tiny whisper of Dad's deep-dimpled smile, and drop it off as you fly past – then maybe it'll lodge deep inside the clavicles of my heart and wriggle around in my cells and platelets and plasma, and then I'll wake up on Christmas morning with my own small smile and full heart, ready to start this crazy ol' Christmas business again: still dad-less, but somehow also full.

Have a good one, Santa – and might I suggest that you treat yourself and Mrs Claus to a good rest, and maybe even a holiday afterwards. And give the elves a bit of a bonus. And the reindeers an extra carrot. I think you all deserve it.

Lotsa love,

Moo xxx

PS: About the microscope. I just remembered it was Dad who gave it to me, not you. I was eight years old, past the Santa stage – so it had to be him. He hid it and wrote me a cryptic poem which I had to decipher in order to find where the microscope was hidden. It took me over an hour to find it while he and Mum slept in. (See? He was a smart man!) And it was so, so, so worth the wait, when I finally did.

Mary Anne Butler: first playwright (ever) to be honoured with the Victorian Prize for Literature

Dear Santa

Our 'grown-up' selves, now known **a**s Poppo and Gaga, are writing to help you remember our **t**wo beautifu**l** grandchildren **a**t Christma**s**. They are At**l**as, who's five, and Juniper, wh**o**'s two. Their family mo**v**ed recently and have a n**e**w address, so plea**s**e don't forget them. We understand how hard it must be to find each and every kid in this huge, crazy world and bring a ray of hope, **j**oy and love to them at Christmas, especially those who may not have a home, a family or anyone to write letters for them, and let yo**u** know where they are. We **n**ever had sisters ourselves, only smelly brothers, so Atlas **i**s a very lucky boy who really loves his little sis and is teaching her hea**p**s of stuff, like building, racing and singing, as w**e**ll as learning to share his toys, guitars, clapping sticks and Spiderman outfits, while hugging and kissing her, usually against he**r** will!

So, dear Santa, hope this finds you well, and you find them as well!!

Love,

Poppo and Gaga xx (KB and Tan xx)

PS As you travel around this earth, could you also sprinkle a little extra compassion, empathy, tolerance and understanding?

Kevin Bennett: singer–songwriter, 'The Flood'

Dear Santa

I have everything I could possibly want in life. I have enough material objects; how could I long for anything? My blessings are overwhelming. So, what can I ask of you?

Would you have any influence in getting rid of Donald Trump? You would be doing me – and the world – a big favour.

Does your power extend to helping persecuted peoples? The Rohingya people of Myanmar have copped a holocaust at the hands of the military – and Aung San Suu Kyi looks complicit, which is horrifying in itself.

Alright, Santa, this is my big one: Tibet. The two words 'genocide' and 'holocaust' apply here too. China walked in and invaded Tibet in 1959. The suffering of Tibetan people knows no limits. This one upsets me the most, Santa, because I see Tibet as the World Storehouse of Religious Wisdom. I believe the Tibetans have best worked out the purpose of life, somewhat due to their (previous) isolation and their unique Himalayan environment. The Chinese have systematically destroyed 1500 years of accumulated wisdom and religious thought. I see this as a crime against humanity, Santa, which will echo down the centuries. Can you have a look at what you can do about Tibet?

Santa, everybody asks you to give them something. May I suggest you take a long break, with Ms Santa if it suits you both, and take time to relax and smell the (Arctic) flowers, or even travel, or take a cruise! You don't want to wear yourself out. A lot of people – kids – are counting on you. Wishing you a long, sturdy and peaceful life – such as the Tibetans enjoyed before 1959.

Greg

Greg 'That's The Thing About Football' Champion: founding member of the Coodabeen Champions

Dear Santa

Please soften the hearts of the hard men. Help them revisit the innocence of childhood, and undo the damage they have done.

Graeme

Graeme Connors: songwriter, wrote 'I'm Married to My Bulldog Mack' for Slim Dusty

Dear Santa

You may not already know that our beautiful sister Jan Holt passed away last week. She was a really good person, and you would never have crossed her off your present list for being naughty ... well, almost never.

Jan spent her working life caring for, advocating for, educating and standing with people living with HIV and AIDS. Starting in Perth in the mid '80s, she watched helplessly as good people dropped like flies. Jan then took up the fight in her home town of Darwin when she returned in 1990.

She was at the coalface of this horrific pandemic and worked tirelessly for over 30 years, until she fell ill a few months ago. That makes her a decent person in my books.

I met her in the '90s. The blonde and voluptuous sweetheart organised events for our small queer community in Darwin. These were fun, inclusive country-style dances where she would promote the latest message, treatment or advice about HIV – always with respect and discretion. I met my life partner at one of these gigs twenty years ago and we are both very grateful.

Santa, she did this all with so much love. She did not deserve to die from liver cancer. That was just wrong and fucking cruel.

Our Jan loved a drink or two or four. So do you, I heard. Guess it's a part of coping with the stress of helping so many people all the time. But still, it's a shitty blow that Jan passed before she could enjoy retirement. Her partner, Andrew, is facing the rest of his life alone. That's plain crappy.

So, Santa, I want to ask for one last present in Jan's honour: get your lazy elves, pixies and that chubby missus of yours up off their asses and make one present for the world. Find a cure for this fucked-up disease soon, please, and y'all can retire too.

I don't want any more pressies from you mob ever again, if it helps.

Love from

David (Daisy) Taylor

David Taylor: The Knockabout Chef, homeless mentor and arts advocate

Dear Santa

I remember when I was around six years old, trying to keep my eyes open into the wee hours of Christmas Eve to catch a glimpse of you as you placed the presents in the pillowcase that I had neatly hung on the fireplace. Every year was the same. I never got to see you but, strangely, I saw my father a few times. I didn't know what he was doing there but he told me he did *not* drink the beer and chips that were left out for you.

As I got older I had to block my ears when my big brothers and sister teased me that you were not real … NOT REAL?! You are kidding me, I saw you in the local store, and even sat on your knee telling you my dreams of a new train set.

Actually, I never got that train set. I didn't get many of the other things I asked you for. One thing I definitely did not ask for was socks, underwear and a new school shirt. How come they kept appearing with monotonous regularity every Christmas morning?

When it became obvious that you were just a figment of my imagination and merely another marketing ploy to hype up children to bug their parents into present-buying submission, I felt a bit silly, used and gullible.

But, true to form, when my son was about six, I crept into his room on Christmas Eve, drank the beer and left some new socks, underwear AND a train set in the pillowcase he had neatly nailed to the fireplace.

See, I eventually got the train set I wanted, and my son loved his new socks.

Graham

Graham 'Buzz' Bidstrup: CEO Jimmy Little Foundation, musician, songwriter, The Angels, Gang Gajang, Party Boys

Dear Santa

As you know, I was a single parent for many years, bringing up my two beautiful sons. Halfway through those years I succumbed to our family disease, renal failure. (This is when your kidneys stop working and you have to go on dialysis.)

My ex-wife had trained as a nurse but hadn't worked for years. After the kids left school and she had a little more time, she decided to retrain and joined the team at the Austin Hospital in Melbourne – funnily enough, in the renal ward where they treat the dialysis patients.

Then one day three years ago, I got a call from my eldest boy and my world came crashing down. He had inherited our family disease and was in end-stage renal failure. This was the worst time of my life – worse than my divorce, worse than my six years on dialysis.

I called his mother and asked what to do. Should I bring him to her hospital? Was this a conflict of interest? What do I do, what do I do?

She demanded I bring him straight to her ward, and in the next four months she hassled her co-workers, the specialists and doctors and did everything she could to get our boy on the transplant list.

This was a side of her that I had never seen. She got herself tested and volunteered to be his kidney donor. Long story short, it was the quickest period in the history of the hospital from diagnosis to successful transplant.

From being my slightly annoying ex-wife, she turned into the hero of our little family and will now be my hero forever.

So, what I want for Christmas is anything that Penny really wants. You know her address.

Over and out,

Brent

Brent Parlane: contemporary singer–songwriter and a conflicted kidney transplant recipient

Dear Santa

I'm going to ignore last year's Cease and Desist, as I have been a particularly good girl this year. Legal action just seemed mean, and I don't even think letter writing counts as stalking. Like I said in court, that wasn't me outside your house, it just looked like me because you wanted it to be.

While I do appreciate your feedback about being over 30, and therefore too old for Santa, I would argue (again) that being in my mid-30s means I am more deserving of gifts than I have ever been.

This year for Christmas I would like the following:

To never again have an occasion to utter the phrase 'I slept weird and now my neck hurts'.

To only have dark circles on my eyes on the day after a bender, not just because I drank seven instead of eight glasses of water the day before.

For my skin specialist to stop being surprised that I, the massive ginger, haven't got a melanoma yet.

For people older than me to stop saying 'just you wait' in an ominous fashion.

For vitamins to be added to instant coffee.

For a patent for the above idea because that is genius but paperwork sucks.

That will do for me, otherwise I'm all good.

Yours truly,

[redacted]

Correctional Facility on behalf of Ange Thompson

PS Oh, and can we get kids out of detention? Might as well ask you, as asking real people isn't working.

Angela Thompson: comedy producer, Renaissance Woman

Dear Santa

I only ask for one thing: that extra eye. It's tough having just the one. Aside from the cosmetic issues, the stares on the street (two-eyed stares, mind you) and the woeful shortage of monocles these days, my depth perception is shot to buggery.

There's no triangulation. I carry a small ruler with me, only able to tell if a car is too close by measuring the perceptible distance between headlights, which is a terrible procedure, especially when driving. Oh, the collisions suffered while consulting the distance chart taped to my dash, organised according to vehicle type, year of manufacture, frequency, I can never remember which. Such pain, misery and absurd insurance premiums, all because I only have this one eyeball. Did I mention that it almost fills the entirety of my cranial cavity? What's up with that?

Just one other thing – bear with me, please. These pointy ears. Can we do something about them? They don't really improve my hearing; I'm not even sure if they *are* ears, or just easy-to-draw angles. They make conventional headphones nearly impossible. Hats, forget it. I've been waiting for stovepipes to come back into fashion – all that lovely tall tuck-space: when oh when will Abe Lincoln chic finally hit its 150-year cyclical peak? Come on hipsters, you're so close! I'm tired of being called donkey or rabbit on the street by all those racist button-eared types. The liberals are even more confronting: '*Are* you a rabbit? *Are* you a donkey? Come join our *support group!*' I don't know which is worse, blunt denigration or this desperate yearning for compassionate inclusion. No wait, I do know.

And this tail. Yes, sure, it's a great counterbalance for the ears (moot if said ears did not exist in the first place) and helps me pivot and climb telephone poles for quick escapes, but really? It's massive! I've seen possums; those are good tails. I've seen spider monkeys, seahorses, chameleons, all of my prehensile kin, and I never hear any one of them asking, 'Does my arse look big in this?' I mean, where did this engorged door sausage come from, an illustrated encyclopaedia of dinosaurs circa 1890? Come on. How about we lose the ears *and* the tail in a package deal. Then I wouldn't need to be scooting up telephone poles in the first place, chased by all those dogs mistaking me for a delicious marsupial.

The claws? Ahem. You try getting a discount manicure with *these* bad boys. And how many times has a potential partner, with a strong emphasis on that eternal adjective *potential*, made a poorly concealed 'ew' sound the moment I take my shoes off to clear the toe jam. It's the claws, I tell you! As if fingernails and toenails aren't claws, you simian hypocrites. I mean, have any of you even been to the zoo? What do you think those things are on the end of your appendages, little shoelace aglets, fingertip pen caps, cosmetic full stops for the elegant syntax of your body and soul? They are just crappy claws, people. You can't even open a can with them. That said, I would like my claws to look more crappy. And learn to use a can-opener, especially in the company of aforementioned potential partners.

There's the hair, the pot belly, the excessive number of canine teeth, the general cartoony outline. God knows how I've tried to wash it off (and I'm assuming God is cc'd on these letters as much as you are cc'd on prayers; even though I get that Santa is an anagram of Satan, I assume it's a private joke between buddies, although I'm still figuring out the 'God – dog' thing, must be hilarious somehow, but I digress): this dicky atonal outline, it's just so *illustrative*. It's not even ironic. I mean, could it just look a bit more naïve or something, like an awkward doodle in a high-school diary or a defiant homemade tattoo rendered with a compass needle and a busted biro, that would be cool. Or a bit more vector graphic, or with smooth 3D CG gradations in digital pastel shades, that stuff will *never* go out of style. This sketchy black pen delineation just looks crap. You call this art? How the hell am I even going to get past security at the Venice Biennale? At least cover me with colourful yarn-balls, scale me up to the size of an ocean liner, immerse me in the combined bodily fluids of a yak, or *something*. Who wants cute drawings, anyway? Some earnest rag desperate for decorative wing-ding space-fillers, with a printing deadline circa last Tuesday.

What? What's this? A hat? A flower? This is your reply? Twee metaphor, huh? Nice one, Santa. Trust me, I know a last-minute scribble fishing for non-existent meaning when

I see one. I get the whole pretentious ruse of creativity, my quasi-mythological friend: I *am* that ruse. Still, it's a lovely flower. Beautiful, really ... Probably missing a petal though. Could we get an extra petal on this thing? I really think this flower needs one more petal.

Yours monoptically,

Critter

Shaun Tan: Head of Miscellaneous Critters, Creatures and Abnormalities at The Stick, *Academy Award-winning illustrator*

Dear Santa

I haven't written to you for many years but thought I'd say, Hi, remember me?

This Christmas I would love no material items. I know everyone says that, but have you looked around and taken in exactly how much stuff we all have? You'd know better than most because I know you've stumbled over all the stuff when you've been delivering toys to my children. We all have enough stuff.

I'd love to say please bring me another pair of boots, but I believe others are more deserving of this and I probably have enough (please don't be too shocked when you read that).

What I would love, and I'm trying not to sound too clichéd here, is for everyone to have enough this Christmas – enough love, enough funds to buy enough for those they care about, enough happiness, enough food, and enough people around them to not feel alone at Christmas.

May everyone be surrounded by love and happiness on Christmas Day and may country music ring through the land

… okay, this may be pushing it, but I know it'll be ringing out from my home.

Thanks for listening, Santa, and I hope I won't leave it as long to write next time. Thanks for all the gifts and for sharing the love throughout the world as you travel faster than the speed of light with those reindeer and kangaroos pulling your sleigh.

May we all be thankful for what we have and find someone to be grateful for each day.

Rebecca

PS Santa, if Patrick and Gracie ask for noisy toys, pretend the letter has been lost in the mail. My sanity thanks you in advance.

Rebecca Belt: country music journo

Dear Santa

I know it has been a while since we talked last, but right now I really feel like I need your help, your guidance and the gift of a lifetime.

Recently I have come to the conclusion that my overall sense of self-esteem is very heavily tied to what other people think about me, and I would really like a gift from you that I believe will help me to address this deeply ingrained issue. For Christmas this year I was hoping that you could please make me famous.

Not that bullshit fame like what people have with Instagram, but real fame, household-name fame – you know, that 'fill the empty hole in your soul' kind of fame. The type of fame where I can't leave my house or travel the world without people recognising me and telling me what a positive impact MY WORK made on THEIR LIVES. But that ultimately results in me hitting a point in my early 40s where I have an existential crisis, I get divorced, I give away the majority of my wealth and sell all my belongings to travel to India. I return some years later with a fully unkempt beard and wearing weird clothing, but it doesn't matter because I have become 'spiritually awakened'.

In exchange for your gift of fame, my promise to you is that I will then return to the limelight in a once-off extremely well-paid *60 Minutes* special and I will share with the world how none of the stuff that I achieved earlier in my life really meant anything.

Only to have Liam Bartlett point out the irony that for me to have a spiritual awakening I had to go through the initial process of getting caught up in the trappings of fame and success. You know, kind of like how Jim Carrey did in *Bruce Almighty* ...

Also, I know it's not politically correct and I really don't want to be seen as the guy who's 'fat-shaming' Santa, but I feel it has to be said. At this point in your life, with your workload and all of your responsibilities, you should take a good hard look at your overall health and wellbeing. Also, I recently got told that you have been looking at me when I am sleeping. What's the go with that? *Suuuuuper* creepy, dude!

Anyways, I am looking forward to your response, not to mention the possibility of filling that truly unfillable void that I have in my heart.

Cheers, Nick,

p.

Paris Mitchell: public speaker

Dear Santa

Just seeing a picture of you makes me smile. I know I'm not the only one. You make me think of giving. And when it comes down to it, they say that giving is the greatest gift.

Something's been on my mind lately, and I would LOVE to have a chat with you about it this Christmas – or maybe we can wait until you're off-season when you have a bit more time. Because I reckon you must have some idea of the big picture of this planet … with all that inter-hemisphere travel up there on your sleigh.

Giving is important. And I sometimes wonder, Santa, do you think some of us could learn how to truly receive? I'm not talking about getting THINGS here. I mean really receiving what we truly need at a deep level, the most important thing being love.

How many of us do you think really know how to receive love? How many of us believe we are worthy of true, unconditional love?

Is it just me, or do you agree that there's something in this? Do you think that if people believed they were worthy of unconditional love, and were able to receive it, that there would be less conflict? Less war? Do you think we would start caring for each other more? And taking actions to sustain the health of our planet, the very thing that gives us life ...?

Thank you for taking the time to read this, Santa, I know you're busy. I'm keen to hear your well-informed, global perspective on how, together, we can set some wheels in motion towards people being able to give and receive love better, and somehow short-circuit the layers of pain and damage that get in the way.

If we were all able to give and receive love fully, this world would be a very different place.

Love and light,

Jodi

Jodi Martin: songwriter – if you love James Taylor or Jack Johnson, you'll love Jodi

Dear Santa

I am hoping you can make my Christmas wishes come true. All I want is some civility. You've always flown around the world with a big smile and looked after other people. By your very actions, you've combined your love of the free market and commercialism with an ability to ensure that the most disadvantaged receive as much as the more fortunate.

When I hear and see people call others bad names, often on all this rubbish social media, I think, *Why can't they be as good as Santa?*

So perhaps this Christmas, as you drop off your presents down all those chimneys around the world, just add a letter reminding us to show respect for each other.

Thanks Santa, from

Ian

Ian Smith AM: influential political lobbyist, married to the far more impressive Natasha Stott Despoja (his words)

Dear Santa

I'm not sure if this will reach you. The Finnish government claims that you are now domiciled at Rovaniemi in Lapland – I have even made my way there to sit on your knee and, having convinced you of my 'nice' status, rolled out a list of desirable gifts that I'd be rather keen to find arrayed before my chimney (which hasn't worked for years – who knows how you squeeze down the bloody thing).

There was a question that I meant to put to you then, in those icy wastes, which has been driving me crazy ever since. And that is: Do you have a profit share arrangement in place for all those songs that use your name to increase sales at Christmas? I mean, it has been going on for a long time, well before the arrival of rock'n'roll, and while I'm sure you've been amused by the great Satchmo, Louis Armstrong, enquiring 'Zat You, Santa Claus?' and Eartha Kitt sending you out a rather seductive entreaty in 'Santa Baby', it is hard to imagine you getting a lot of joy out of something like Michael Bolton telling all and sundry that 'Santa Claus is Coming to

Town' (I'd like to think that Bruce Springsteen is more likely to float your boat – or at least lift your sled – with that selection … or perhaps the Crystals on Phil Spector's Christmas album might have impressed your jolly red self with their rather bombastic treatment).

If you are not getting your slice out of this, then you need to get a new agent (I can suggest a few names). This agent could even represent others in your rather exclusive stable. It is hard to estimate how much might have accrued. Who knows what might be owed to your chief transportation manager, in particular! 'Rudolph the Red-Nosed Reindeer' has been doing the rounds since Gene Autry, Spike Jones and Bing Crosby invaded the hit parades with it in 1950. I hate to tell you this, but certain disreputable children have been known to take outrageous liberties with the words, even shouting them loudly. The disrespect is abominable. However, I can't imagine that your associate Frosty the Snowman is in a position to raise much of a fuss. He's prone to meltdown, I believe.

Now, I have to admit to having entertained a few cheeky musical outings myself, Your Frostiness. My ready accommodation of all things pertaining to the silly season manifests itself in bizarre forms. Chief among them is a vast collection of seasonal recordings – hundreds upon hundreds of cheery ditties graced with bells, chimes and innumerable 'ho ho hos'. Around my house on Christmas Eve has been heard the not-always-lilting tones of 'Santa and the Purple People Eater' by Sheb Wooley; 'Santa Claus, Go Straight to the Ghetto' by James Brown; 'Sock it to Me, Santa' by Bob Seger, 'I Was a Teenage Reindeer' by Jim 'Mr Magoo' Backus; 'Santa and the Sidewalk Surfer' by the Turtles; 'A Surfer's Christmas List' by the Surfaris; 'Put the Loot in the Boot, Santa' by Mae West; 'Santa Claus and His Old Lady' by Cheech & Chong; 'Santa Claus is Watching You' by Ray Stevens; 'Santa Claus and Popcorn' by Merle Haggard; 'Dear Mr Claus' by Paul Revere & the Raiders; 'Hey Santa!' by the Brian Setzer Orchestra; 'Santa Doesn't Cop Out on Dope' by Martin Mull; and, if you'll pardon the presumption, Frankie Valli of the Four Seasons trilling high on 'I Saw Mommy Kissing Santa Claus'. (Best, for the sake of your domestic harmony, that they left that one out of *Jersey Boys*). Oh yes, a very definite threat to your personal safety is 'I'm Gonna Lasso Santa Claus' by Brenda Lee, though she is so small I wouldn't take the threat too seriously.

Now I don't know if you are inclined to blush under that beard, but a rather audacious lady called Cyndi Lauper, known for declaring that girls just want to have fun among other pursuits, was proposing altogether too much fun with 'Minnie and Santa'. She let her true colours show with this raunchy outing, where Minnie promises to be 'laying in wait on a bear skin rug' for your good self, wearing 'a bright red bow'. I'm almost blushing myself. It has been said that this festive song has the unique distinction of being the only time in history that the phrase 'cookies and milk' has sounded downright lascivious. I'm not sure if you have internet access in your workshop but it may be best that you don't check that one out. And certainly keep yourself distant, along with the good lady Claus and all those helpful little elves, from 'Back Door Santa' by Clarence Carter and, more recently, Bon Jovi. The essence of this salacious song is that one shouldn't leave one's woman alone when Santa comes to town. (Given the territorial range you service, I couldn't imagine you'd have enough time to mount a real threat.) Clarence and Bon Jovi warned, 'I make all the little girls happy while the boys are out to play' and reminds householders to lock their chimney up tight on Christmas Eve. The liberty!

I'm sure I'm not telling you anything you don't know when I say that a number of these songs are rendered on disc, on television specials, at candlelight gatherings in parks and shopping centres and (not that often) in churches and cathedrals. No ordinary pop ditties seem to have the hold, adaptability and the awesome longevity of this elite handful of musical works. Pop and rock acts perform them, but so too do blues, country, jazz, reggae, folk, soul, R'n'B, punk, alternative, cabaret and world music artists.

The real explosion – if you'll forgive an amateur like me telling you how to suck eggs (or at least partake of those aforementioned milk and cookies) – came about through a shameful incident early in December 1957, when disc jockey Al Priddy in the American city of Portland eagerly rushed to air a track from the fourth album by the hottest chart sensation in the land. Within minutes of the song hitting the airwaves, Priddy was out of a job for having played 'material of extremely bad taste'. The record was *Elvis' Christmas Album*, stacked mostly with tender treatments of seasonal and spiritual chestnuts. The Portland reaction was not an isolated incident; stations all over America were banning the album in outrage. It was almost as if this swivel-hipped hooligan had set fire to the flag and spurned his mum's apple pie. It didn't help that Elvis Presley had tendered a request to you in the form of 'Santa Bring My Baby Back to Me' (as if he couldn't get out on the prowl himself, in his pink Cadillac).

As tame as Elvis's festive offering was, it stands as a watershed for what has become one of the most active and profitable genres of popular music (possibly to your detriment). Those hapless DJs did not lose their air shifts for nought; they were instrumental in ushering in a fascinating rock/pop genre. Since that monumental Christmas of 1957, virtually every contemporary music entity of any consequence has cut a December ditty – many of them citing your good self. In fact it would be easier to cite those who *haven't* than those who have.

I should declare here, old fellow, that I am also a culprit. Back in 1976, as the creator and manager of a triple-platinum rock group called Ol' 55, I came up with the lyrics for a song called '(I Want A) Rockin' Christmas'. The words, scrawled on an aircraft sick bag in true rock'n'roll tradition, were hardly poetry: 'Listen to me, Santa, won't you bring my lover to me. Wrapped up in ribbons and dropped down my chim-in-ey'. Nonetheless the song became a huge national smash hit. Do forgive me, I meant no offence, truly. Would it help my case if I sang a refrain of 'Santa Claus (I Still Believe In You)' by Alabama?

You know, there seems no barrier, musical, religious or cultural, to participation in this genre. The proudly Jewish Barbra Streisand has recorded an entire Christmas album, while Bob Dylan has just done the same. They give out awards these days for such interfaith gestures (though I'm not entirely sure if that word applies here). We're just glad you're around and that your back holds up as you streak through the skies lugging our computer upgrades, BMX bikes, Barbie and Ken dolls with all their detachable parts, roller skates and, in my case, neat hats to help cover my long-ago-receded hairline.

All the very best.

Glenn

PS Keep thinking about that agent idea.

PPS Expect me back in Ravaniemi some time. I hope your leg has got better.

PPPS I've been VERY nice this year. I'm forwarding my list. How are you with airline upgrades?

Glenn A Baker AM: rock journalist, commentator, author and broadcaster

Dear Santa

Nice try. Like I'm going to tell YOU what I want for Christmas. You've got scammer written all over you, phishing for personal information so you can choke my feed with ads for good-quality chocolate and, I don't know, chicken tattoos and a new car. There is no upside to me telling you 'What I want'. Being an adult means my needs cannot be met by a bulging stocking on Christmas day. Material objects do not fix the screaming existential habdabs or address the void. One day I will die. What are you going to do about that?

And, frankly, it is no longer in the Zeitgeist for older cis males straining against their red velvet suits to be asking anyone a) to sit on their knee, b) if they've been 'good', whatever *that* means (*ugh!*), or c) to whisper in their ear, your grey beard tickling their lobes, that you'll bring them expensive gifts.

Seriously, dude, you're rocking a predator vibe. It's not cool.

Sure, this is a bummer. There was a time when Santa was seen as comforting and fun, and one of my fondest Christmas memories is from when I was about ten, when my parents bought me a large inflatable Father Christmas and left it at the bottom of my bed to wake up to. I was genuinely thrilled and spent two days with my arms wrapped around him as I watched TV or read a book, but you could also see it as pretty sad, given that I was an only child with no friends apart from Prince the golden retriever. Prince may also have been dead by this point. When you're going back this far in time, chronology becomes shaky.

But my point? Times change. Whatever you're putting down no one is picking up. You're a poster boy for paternalism and white privilege – just another Caucasian middle-aged male who thinks throwing money at a problem makes it go away, and that everyone wants what's in his sack. And, come on, you bring presents for 'boys' and 'girls'? Nice one. Have you even *heard* of gender fluidity?

I can't even.

Santa. Baby. You know what I want for Christmas? For you to wake up Christmas morning 'woke'.

Season's greetings,

Fiona

PS: Where's your wife? Why do we never see her? It's all about you, isn't it? Misogynist prick.

Fiona Scott-Norman: journo, DJ, Big Issue *stalwart*

Dear Santa

What the fuck was with you, Santa?

We were all told we loved you. We weren't asked, we were told. 'You love Santa! All kids love Santa! Remember all that stranger danger stuff? Forget it. Sit on this rando's knee and answer anything he asks. And smile for the camera.'

Santa, you are a creepy old guy who looks different every time, wears the most crooked outfit ever, has a sex pest beard, never ages, lives in the North Pole with 'elves' (read: GIMPS), and who makes toys with such a keen eye for detail they even replicate the Kmart price tags.

Holy fuck, my childhood was full of harmful, nonsensical bullshit: Jesus, God, the Holy Spirit, Easter Bunny, Tooth Fairy, ghosts, monsters, haunted houses, if you step on the crack you'll break your mother's back, and you can't go swimming for an hour after you've eaten or you'll die of cramp. None of it made any sense yet we were supposed to apply logic and reason when it came to sibling relationships, road rules, mathematics and household chores.

No offence, mate, but if I had my time again I wouldn't do the Santa thing with my kids. I wasn't comfortable with the lying and the promoting of 'if you're good you will get presents' and 'there's a man watching you all the time' stuff.

Regretfully, I did the Santa stuff with my kids. I didn't do the 'if you're good' and 'he is watching you' bullshit, but it's everywhere else and impossible to avoid. 'He's making a list and checking it twice, he's gonna find out who's naughty and nice ...'

To my shame I didn't even think about it at the time. I hated the extra pressure of ascertaining what they wanted, buying it, hiding it, tiptoeing out when they were asleep and not getting caught. I most definitely did not like some magic man getting credit for my hard work.

There's nothing like Santa to teach a kid about privilege and unfairness. Some kids get lots of presents; others get not so many. Some wake on Christmas Day to nothing at all. Believing in Santa trains kids in cognitive dissonance, which is harmful and destructive. As they get older, they start to wise up and things don't add up as we continue to lie and/or not tell them the truth.

Like bringing children up with religion, the whole Santa thing is manipulative and deceptive. Of course, kids grow out of Father Christmas, the Easter Bunny and the Tooth Fairy, and the smart/lucky ones grow out of the damaging God bullshit, but still, what is a child to think when their parents lie to their face repeatedly?

I imagine they think, as I did, 'What else did you bullshit to me about and why?'

I'm not asking for anything, Santa, I just had to get this off my chest.

Thanks for reading, sorry it's been so long. Hope you are well.

Dev

Catherine Deveny: risk-taker, untamed brumby, mainstream media pariah

Dear Santa

It has been some time since I last wrote to you and I hope you don't mind me reconnecting with you at this later stage in my life. I'm not sure what your policy is on the age of the author of the letters you receive, but after all, pretty much all grown-ups (as you would call us) still feel like kids at heart.

I have a small favour to ask of you, and I'm hoping you still have the ability to make a wish come true. As a father of four wonderful children now, I can understand why you can't always deliver all presents listed on a child's Christmas list, but I also imagine that would depend on how long their list was.

I pretty much remember every list I ever wrote to you, and I'm also pretty sure my parents forwarded all my lists to you on my behalf. My parents came from very little money and as a result suggested that I keep my Christmas lists down to a few items that meant a lot to me, but were not worth a lot of money.

Like most children, I wasn't always the best at listening to instructions from my parents, but when the instructions concerned how to order presents from Santa at Christmas, trust me, you listen up and toe the line, and that's what I did. I can assure you my lists weren't ever that long or of great financial value (with the exception of the Mongoose BMX bike that I requested in 1984 and did not receive).

The only reason I have felt the need to get back in communication with you after all these years is because last week I attended an '80s music trivia night to raise funds for a new 'lonely chair' and a new netball ring for my children's school. (A lonely chair, if you don't know, is for a child to sit on in the playground if they have no one to play with. Other kids are encouraged to include them in their games. And I assume you know what a netball ring is.)

As I walked into the '80s-decorated hall, hanging from the centre of the ceiling, fashioned out of cardboard, was a massive Rubik's Cube. Its sole purpose was to act as decoration for the themed fundraiser, but it did much more than that for me that night. It transported me back to a time in my youth when this small, yet ever-so-effective and complicated square puzzle became an icon of an era, a symbol of my youth, if you will. But why, at the age of 48, was I so drawn to this dodgy, parent-made, six-coloured box, swinging from a piece of string above my head? And then it dawned on me. It was because I never had one. And do you know why I never had one? Because you never gave it to me. In essence, well actually in fact, I was disappointed all over again.

Then it all started flooding back to me, the Evel Knievel stunt bike, the G.I. Joe action figure, the Stretch Armstrong doll (and of course the Mongoose BMX bike with red skyway tuffs). I got none of them. I mean, let's be honest here. You had one job – albeit multiplied by the population of the youth of the planet, but it's still one job – to make kids happy by supplying the key items on a list.

Would it really have been that hard to throw a Rubik's Cube into my present bag?

I'm not necessarily suggesting your heart is as cold as the area you live in, but I started thinking about the presents that my children are getting these days. And even if I factor in CPI, my kids and pretty much all their friends are well ahead of where my friends and I were at their age, as far as the yield of gifts they are receiving is concerned.

In the current climate (I mean the political environment, not the temperature one) it's worth noting that in Australia we replace prime ministers almost on a daily basis. This is by no means a threat, but you should NOT consider your job as a guaranteed position. I could easily start a spill within your own ranks.

Some of the major positions in the world are now not even skills-based appointments. Have you seen who's running America at the moment? So, we could potentially get anyone to do your job if you're not careful.

What is my request? Well, quite simply, I wish to resurrect and resubmit part of my 1984 Christmas list (with the exception of the Mongoose BMX bike, of course) – not all of the items on my 1984 list, not even some of them, just one of them: the goddamn Rubik's Cube.

Yes, I am aware that I can without doubt now afford to buy one for myself, but it's not the same as getting it from you. We are not supposed to buy ourselves a Christmas present. We are supposed to be given them by Santa. And that's you, mate.

So here I go, I am going to ask just one more time … Dear Santa, could I please have a Rubik's Cube for Christmas?

I sincerely hope that this letter finds its way in front of your eyes, but more importantly, I hope it is read by your heart.

Kind regards,

Shane

A broken-hearted boy who's a man.

PS I pretty much know where you live. (That was definitely a threat.)

Shane Jacobson: 'dunny man' turned actor

Dear Santa

Doubtless you receive correspondence of this nature far too often. First of all, I'd like to apologise for not keeping in touch. It has been remiss of me not to write to you since, if memory serves, 1976, when I asked you for a totem tennis set, a Dinky Toys die-cast model of SHADO 2 from the Gerry Anderson TV series *UFO*, and a vinyl copy of ABBA's seminal album *Arrival*. All of which arrived safely, thank you. That was a red-letter day for me, as I think I mentioned in a brief follow-up letter. I was (admittedly) tardy in that response, but in my defence, I was starting to not believe in you by that stage. Apologies for that, also.

I hope this helps explain why I never wrote to thank you for *Hooked on Classics Vol 2* after your visit in 1981. I was fifteen, and I'm sure you'd know from bitter experience that getting a fifteen-year-old to believe in you is a big ask. More is the pity, which I say with the benefit of hindsight. But let's move on.

For the sake of clarity (as I am sure there are a lot of people on your mailing list, and you have a lot of fish to fry, so to speak), I am the Matthew Saville formerly of 38 South Esplanade, Glenelg South, South Australia, 5025. You would probably remember the terracotta-tiled roof and the lack of chimneys. That must've been a difficult obstacle for you, and I am keenly aware that you work on a tight schedule. On that evening, particularly.

I want to say, admittedly (again) with the benefit of hindsight, that I really appreciated the fruits of your annual visits, back in the day, and remain greatly impressed that you invariably managed to locate, and make your silent and undisrupted way, to the bottom of our tree in the rumpus room, given that Glenelg is a palindrome and always goes to some weird autocorrect whenever I type it into Google Maps. (Not sure if you've ever encountered that problem; gosh I really hope not! That Rudolph must have an incredible sense of direction, man. Please pass on my kindest regards if you are still in contact/working together.)

I digress.

This may surprise you, but the reason I've (finally) decided to contact you after all these years, even though I understand that my sons, Ben and Charley, remain devoted votaries and have asked me to pass on their fondest regards to both you and Mrs Claus, isn't to put the hard word on you. I'm not asking for another premiership for the Western Bulldogs, or for a new or near-new Subaru Outback, or, I should stress, an AACTA nomination this year (although any of the above would be nice, and greatly appreciated). No, sir. I write because I want to help you. I would like to assist in the great, rightly celebrated service that you provide. If I may. I know, that's an arrogant position, but there it is.

I would like to help you with the list(s) you are making ATM. By that I mean 'At the Moment', not 'Automatic Teller Machine' (another hint, there, Christmas-present-wise).

Again, I digress.

For the sake of brevity, which I freely admit isn't one of my strong points, I've focused my attention on Australian politicians, and/or people who work, directly or indirectly, in the Australian political landscape. Some of these names may already be familiar to you, but I invite you to revisit them and include them on your list. And, if necessary, check them twice.

Here we go. Mind your step.

Peter Dutton (naughty). I'm sure you've heard of this guy. He started a spill with the Coalition's leadership. Ultimately, he was usurped by someone called Scott Morrison, who now leads the country, despite the fact that we hadn't heard boo from him prior to the announcement of the spill. Scott likes God and keeping children in detention, which seems a mixed message. Peter, as you know, also enjoys giving unfortunate soundbites to Sydney 'shock jocks' and resembling carbohydrates (read: potatoes). But the main reason you should check your list at least twice regarding the Honourable Minister for Home Affairs is because he started this mess. You can google how terrible it has grown. If you have to give Dutton something, give him the leadership. One more spill in the Coalition won't bother anyone down here, really. I could go on, but it's probably best if you just google him. You'll see.

Malcolm Turnbull (line call, but naughty). I'm calling him 'naughty' because even though he seems okay as a person, he proved to be something of a disappointment as prime minister. I thought he was fine when he got in, because he initially seemed willing to open a discussion about, say, climate change, but it never happened, so maybe he got carpeted by his backbenchers. Who knows? The outcome was pretty straightforward, though. He ended up with lots of mediocre outcomes, on a range of issues. IMHO, if you're putting yourself full forward, you just can't do that. If you want to lead, lead. Go off the front foot. This, I know, requires some hard decisions that might not please your cabinet or your constituency. But that's the barbecue. The Americans describe this notion as 'being presidential'. If you must put something in Malcolm's pillowcase, try some balls. Give him a matching pair of testicles. He might find them useful in later life. (Although it's probably a moot point by now.) If you can't fit any testicles in your sack, maybe you could give him some schadenfreude.

Gina Rinehart (naughty). This was a hard one, because I also harbour a great deal of pity for her. What do you give the woman who already has everything? More lobby groups? Parental approval? Love?

Scott Morrison (naughty). See above.

Robert (Bob) Katter/Senator Fraser Anning (naughty). Once again, google them. Fraser has pretty consistently expressed some unfortunate opinions about people less fortunate than himself, and Mr Katter doubled down on his behalf.

Penny Wong (nice). Google.

Hannah Gadsby (nice). Not sure you're across this, but she made a seismic change this year. Gender stuff, mostly. Maybe by accident, it bulls-eyed the Zeitgeist. Either way, it was a good thing. Give her a T2 gift voucher; she'd like that. Tea is her bag.

Richard Harris and Craig Challen (nice). These guys prove to be the exception to my rule because they're not directly or indirectly involved in politics. They are cave divers. That's their bag. Which one is which escapes my memory, but one's an anaesthetist and the other is a vet. They're members of a diving group called the Wet Mules. They helped save a baker's dozen Thai kids from a flooded cave. Gift idea for them would be socks and jocks, probably. They'd be happy with that, unlike Gina. Socks and jocks would be an insult to her, because of her wealth.

Mister Claus (or Saint Nicholas, or whatever 'handle' you go by these days), I beg you to digest the above, in the sentiment it has been presented. Which is as a suggestion rather than a recommendation. I have no intention of treading on your toes. You are very good at your job, and I, for one, don't want to tell you how to do it.

I trust this letter finds you well. Safe travels on the 24th, big guy. Season's greetings, and kindest regards to you and Mrs Claus.

Matthew

Matthew Saville: AACTA Award-winning TV director

Dear Santa

Hi! Luke McGregor here. My current home doesn't have a chimney so I'm happy for you to use the front or back door, or a window, this year. As far as what do I want for Christmas – I'm not sure, to be honest. A slide big enough for adults would be good, but I'm not sure where I'd put it. I play a lot of video games, so I guess … more video games? I'd have to send you a list of what I already have so there's no double-up. Most of the ones I want haven't been released yet – and I fear the Final Fantasy VII remake will never come out … If it does, though, please deliver that as soon as possible.

I really thought that if I ever wrote a public letter to you it'd be profound but instead I asked for a slide and the Final Fantasy VII remake … I would also like World Peace.

Regards,

Luke

Luke McGregor: comedian and actor

Dear Santa

My dad died a couple of years ago.

Whoa, settle down, I'm not asking you or your elves to do any kooky shit. I know you and your team don't bring dads back from the dead, but if you can, bring back someone else's dad. Mine was ready to go, even though we weren't ready to say goodbye. He left no business undone. No loving words unspoken. He was a ripper. I'm just so grateful we had him when we did. So, let him stay wherever he is, even though when I think about his great gentleness it makes me cry.

Don't get impatient, Santa, I'm getting there. Geez, you'd think with all those jabbering kids you've had on your lap you'd be used to people not getting to the point. At least I haven't weed on you yet. But I see you're getting antsy, so here it is:

I would like IMAGINATION to be in all of our stockings this Christmas, please. (And no, it's not because I think you're a cheapskate, even though when I was five you got me a robot and the lights didn't even light up!)

Here's why. My dad told me (obviously before he died, I'm not nuts), 'Rob, we don't even know what problems we as a species are going to have to solve but I truly believe we can only solve them if as many people, in as many places, are able to live imaginatively.'

Here's the curve ball, Santa. My dad was a politician! A Liberal politician! I know … who ever heard of a politician thinking like this? And right now, with what's going on, it's seriously hard to imagine, but it's true. The last thing he asked himself before he ever made a decision that would affect peoples' lives was: 'Does this help people to be more imaginative, or stop people being imaginative?' If it didn't help, he wouldn't do it, wouldn't say it. If it did help, he'd get on with it as fast as he bloody could.

Isn't it nice to know some leaders think like this? Because to be IMAGINATIVE you have to feel secure; you have to be loved; you have to feel trust in those around you; you have to think for yourself; you have to be brave; you have to persevere; you have to feel okay with contradictions. It's complex. But if IMAGINATION is everyone's goal, a lot of the yukky stuff falls away. Stuff like nasty talk, judgement, division, trolling. None of that helps IMAGINATION flourish.

Now Santa, if you can put IMAGINATION in everyone's stocking, here's what I'll do. (I won't promise to be good, you've been lied to a million times before on that front.) I'll promise to try my best to make sure my home, with my fourteen-year-old twin boys and my beautiful wife, is a place where everyone can be as imaginative as possible, too. It's not easy. Especially with your kids. You want them to succeed, you want them to be polite, you want them to strive. But so often in attempting to ensure that, you demand, you admonish, you direct ... It can feel right, but I'm pretty sure that's not where IMAGINATION lives.

So, it's a tough one, Santa, but it can be done. I've seen it done. My dad did it. He did it for his country. He did it at home as well. When the great politician got home from Canberra there was never a ripple in the house, never a change of mood, just a warmth and the smell of his suits and his soft hands and his gentle voice and his kind blue eyes, because he knew that for people to be imaginative they need their own space just to be.

So please, Santa, give us all IMAGINATION this Christmas; give us our space to be.

Rob

Rob Carlton: Logie Award winning actor (played Kerry Packer in Paper Giants)

Dear Santa

Long ago, when I was a child, after many years of watching Christmas Day turn into the year's cruellest and final insult, my brother Sunny invented his own imaginary day on the 27th of December. That day is known to us as Parrot Day. Parrot Day is a mental day off. There are no presents required, just your presence. And if you don't feel like turning up, that's even better and totally understandable.

To see an actual parrot on this day is the best outcome. Without even realising it you're out in the wild or searching the skies for these beautiful mysteries. One can expect to experience a powerful glimmer of hope for the year ahead once a positive parrot sighting has been confirmed.

Parrot Day cannot and will not be commercialised. It would be nice if people did realise that there is a healthy alternative that hasn't been deep-fried within an inch of its life.

I do not trust or expect that you will help me out, Santa. As well as your name being an anagram for 'Satan', I've always regarded you as being very mischievous and a bit of a deviant.

I now have three small children of my own and trust that you will leave any intended Xbox deep in the bowels of the North Pole.

Thank you!

Parrot Day, the 27th of December! Every year.

Yours truly,

Gus

Gus Leunig: artist, musician, good bloke

Dear Santa

It's been, what, 30 years? Time does fly.

Before I ask for anything I feel like I should explain my lack of correspondence. There's no kind way of saying this, but I stopped writing to you because I found too many fun things to do with actual people.

I was just about to write a letter to you one day, then Jodie G said I could kiss her under the willow near the bike track and Kai asked me about it and Mr Bishop said he could teach me how to shoot three-pointers and then I started wrestling with my friend Barton and before I knew it I was forty.

You must have some decades like that.

Anyway, I'm back writing to you because a lot of the actual people I got so busy with seem to be turning into chatbots or digital assistants or near-field communicators or automatically generated emails or algorithmic music selectors or non-playable characters. Things are okay at the moment, but I think I have all the robots in my life I can handle, so I was wondering this Christmas if you could stop the growth of automation and AI for me? If that's not possible, perhaps you could just let the greengrocer on my road and the fat Polynesian bus driver who sings quietly to himself on the 333 stay human until next Christmas?

I think I've been good, although it's quite hard to tell these days. I haven't pinched my sister in years and am usually pretty quiet in shops, but I do eat meat and dairy and really enjoyed the World Cup, despite knowing about the East Asian slaves who were dying of exhaustion on Qatari construction sites in preparation for the next World Cup.

Truth be told, I'll probably watch that World Cup, too. Also, if it's a trade-off between watching the World Cup and the Polynesian bus driver staying human, I'll probably take the World Cup, so maybe I haven't been as good as I think I've been.

Anyway, anything you can do for me would be appreciated, and I hope that the reindeer aren't bothered too much by the heat up there in the North Pole.

Love,

Ben

Ben Mckelvey: bestselling author, journo and another good bloke

Dear Santa

Jeremy here. Been a while. I'm the kid who tried to catch you on multiple occasions, laying Wile E Coyote-style booby traps around the house on Christmas Eve. Maybe you found them charming; maybe you found them irritating and/or slightly psychotic. To be honest, I wouldn't blame you. Either way, apologies for the trip-wires. Truth is, I just really wanted to meet you. I'm your number-one fan.

I owe you a lot, man. You gave me my Gobo Fraggle Rock doll, who was my constant companion for years. You didn't judge me when I asked for a Care Bear instead of cricket gear. You gave me Lego and a He-Man action figure and were the only adult who actively encouraged my burgeoning sugar addiction.

It's easy for people to shit on you these days. 'Santa's such a creep,' they say. 'That judgemental sell-out thinks he can mess up *my* chimney, eat *my* cookies and tell *me* if I've been naughty or nice? Uh-uh. Fuck him *and* the reindeer he flew in on.' Maybe they have a point. Let's be honest, Santa, the whole sneaking-into-people's-houses-in-the-dead-of-night shtick is all a bit passé.

Like I said, though, I owe you a lot, so this year I thought we could shake things up a bit. This year, I'd like to offer *you* a gift: my advice. I know what you're thinking. 'Advice? From *this* guy? He's 36, he still can't grow a proper beard, and he sometimes plays Nintendo with his feet for an extra challenge.' Fair points, Santa, but I'm not the one who spends 364 days a year stuck in the North goddamn Pole with a bunch of slave-elves and possessed snowmen, so let's not pretend you're better than me. With that in mind, let's begin. *Queer Eye for That Santa Guy!*

First off, the clothes. Don't be afraid to mix things up a bit, man. Relax. Surely whatever contract you signed with Coca-Cola back in the '50s or whatever has expired by now, and even if it hasn't, fuck it. You're Santa. You can do whatever the hell you want. Apparently French tucks are pretty great, so if I were you I'd whip out the odd tailored shirt now and then. Introduce a few more colours to your wardrobe, too. Maybe a nice sky blue to bring out the colour of your eyes? And why not try a nice pair of slim-fit jeans? Show off them pins! (Side note: never touch the beard. She's thriving, and yes, I'm kinda jealous.)

Second, go easy on the beer. Let's say you visit a million households in one night. Yeah, yeah, you visit more than that, but we both know I'm terrible at maths so let's keep things simple. Most of these households offer you milk and cookies, but I'm damn sure a lot of them – like my family – offer you an alcoholic beverage or two with your Tim Tams. Even if only a quarter of households do this, that's still 250,000 beers in one night. That's a lot of beer, Santa. No judgement here, but a lot of children look up to you. Calm down.

Third, we all know you're in possession of some kind of time-travel device. The *whole* world in one night? That's pretty amazing. And don't give me any of that 'it can only freeze time' nonsense. Way I see it, a device that powerful could only come from Father Time, and if you're in cahoots with that crazy cat then anything's possible.

If you can freeze time, you can sure as hell travel back and forward through time, too. You could go back and see Egypt during the reign of Rameses II! You could witness the Big Bang! You could jump forward, read about your own demise, and spend the next however-many years cheating death!

Never be afraid to treat yourself, Santa. Have fun. You deserve it. And hey, if you happen to go back to the Cretaceous period to see the dinosaurs – I'm just spit-balling here – maybe you could bring me back a pet Ankylosaurus. That'd be pretty great.

Like, really great. Really, *really* great.

Look, the point is, this year I'd like a pet Ankylosaurus. Thanks so much!

Your pal,

Jeremy

Jeremy Lachlan: debut author who, as yet, has won no writing prizes but he did once take home $100 in a karaoke competition

Dear Santa

All I ever did was want things from you, which seems pretty rude in retrospect. Hopefully you understand: there were so many things to want and no ways to get them. I didn't have an income, I couldn't go to the shops because I didn't know how to drive a manual, and I was also about two feet tall. We didn't really go to church so you were my God. Well, you, Dad, Mum, my school principal (whom I once called 'Mum', even though he was a man, and clearly not my mum), the lady at the milk bar. Oh, and John from *Playschool*.

I asked a friend once, while I was mid-swing on the monkey bars, 'Do you think anybody ever asks Santa what *he* wants for Christmas?'

She rolled her eyes and with a hand on her hip, said, 'The elves just give him what he wants, whenever he wants it. Der.' She said 'der' a lot, come to think of it.

Your yearly visit was the point of my whole life so by the time Christmas Eve rolled around I'd be hitting peak excitement levels. I devised elaborate plans to tucker myself out on the day. I jumped on the trampoline & kicked the footy & threw tennis balls & did chin-ups & skipped rope & played hopscotch & rollerskated & did Rocky montages & yabbied & commando-rolled & ran & ran & ran. It never worked. I always woke up around two am on Christmas morning, vibrating with the knowledge that there were only a couple of rooms separating me from you.

Eventually I'd sneak into my little brother's room and wake him up, and we'd whisper loudly to each other till we were allowed to wake everyone else up. That early-morning Christmas air was so rich with possibility. We almost couldn't stand it. What would Santa give us that'd make us into new people, better ones than we were this year, better ones than we were *ever*?

HOW CAN ANYONE IN THEIR RIGHT MIND SLEEP RIGHT NOW, I'd whisper loudly to my little brother, who I'd just woken from a deep sleep.

I KNOW, he'd say dutifully, yawning, holding his eyes open with his fingers.

I left my older brother out of it, because he seemed way too wise from the moment I knew him. He addressed the whole Santa thing with a lovely, polite indifference. He never wanted anything. Which was good because he mostly just got a lot of socks. I wish I was more like him (well, apart from all the sock-getting). I wish I could say I wrote to you and said, 'All I want for Christmas, dearest Santa, Sir, Your Highness, is world peace, my family to live long, prosperous lives, and the rescuing of all turtles everywhere.' But you and I both know this is not even slightly true. Me, I wanted everything.

Curiously, I can't really remember what you so generously gave me now. There are some vague, treasured memories: a subscription to *TV HITS*. My very own netball. A tape to learn Italian. *Baby-sitter's Club Summer Special #5*. A voucher to get my ears pierced (still the best day of my life). A tennis racquet bag like the rich kids had. I regularly carried it around the house on my shoulder, for no real reason other than if I let it out of my sight it might just disappear into thin air.

These days, 'Getting Things' has lost a bit of its magic,* and the things I feel powerless to 'get' are also different: the ending of oppression; the dismantling of patriarchy and white supremacy; Christmas songs to be played in shops from mid-December only. People to be better to each other, to not blow each other up, to not be dickheads in general. People I love to come back from the dead, and people I love to never, ever, ever die as long as I'm alive.

To be honest, I miss you a little. I miss those early-morning moments with my little brother. I miss my older brother's gentle patience with us. I miss Mum's smile from the couch as we emptied our Santa sack – a smile I now recognise to be knowing (spoiler alert: SHE WAS WORKING WITH SANTA). I miss Dad filming us with that hulking video camera he'd borrow from work for Christmas every year. I miss the feeling of being surprised by magic, but not being surprised at all, because it was just a fact that it existed. I can't remember the last time I couldn't sleep because I was too excited about something and not worried about everything. I miss believing in you.

Has anyone ever asked you what you believe in? You can write back and tell me, if you like.

With love for you and all turtles everywhere,

Brooke

*Having said that, waving your credit card over that PayPass machine is a kind of magic, I think. A little too magic. A suspicious kind of magic. Seriously, how does that even work. Don't tell me. The way I keep a little magic in my life is that I don't know how anything works.

Brooke Davis: novelist, bike rider and good egg

Dear Santa

As you know, this is my first-ever letter to you. As the youngest of four boys, my childhood belief in your existence was cut short (see also the Easter Bunny, Tooth Fairy and all other benevolent mythological beings).

Instead, my siblings gave me vivid proof of the real (and proximate) existence of vampires, evil clowns and a wide array of terrifying creatures who would haunt my childhood (and, sadly, some years since). To be fair, Stephen King also had a hand in this, but that's beside the point.

Learning now that you do actually exist, and have been delivering my gift each year, I think it's fair to reflect on some of your choices. Overall, you've been off the mark. For example, remember that remote-controlled all-terrain vehicle in 1984? Admittedly, it sounds great in theory, and I was really excited when I tore off the wrapping paper. But a few things undermined your selection:

- First, the batteries were – as always – not included.

- Secondly, a 30cm cord connected the controller to the vehicle (ie it isn't 'remote controlled' if you have to chase after it).
- Lastly (and most importantly) the fact that my older brother received a Commodore 64 computer.

Now, I can forgive the first two. You've got a lot of gifts to give, so it's hard to pay attention to all the details. But the last one was a real kick in the teeth. I mean, the whole thing about you noticing who'd been good? Look, I wasn't perfect, but my brother was definitely worse (see aforementioned vampires, evil clowns, etc).

Year after year, such discrepancies between behaviour and reward became more obvious, especially among my friends. I quickly learned that 'being good' didn't guarantee anything in return – often the opposite was true. And it also seemed like the children of wealthy parents got the best gifts, irrespective of how mean-spirited they might be.

So my wish to you now? How about you try telling kids the truth. Being good doesn't mean they'll get good presents – actually, getting presents isn't even what being good is about. It's really about showing kindness to others, and improving their world (and yours), little by little.

And if all this seems a bit too earnest, then how about a Commodore 64 instead?

Better late than never.

Mark

Mark Brandi: Australia's own Italian-born bestselling crime writer

Dear Santa

As you know, there was the shadow, on Christmas Day last year.

Me, visiting my parents, a few hours south of Perth. Dad reading on the beach. Mum on her new stand-up paddleboard. Me on another. Water swimming-pool clear. A hot breeze pushing us out to sea.

Then the shadow, over the sand. One that wasn't there before. Me, turned shoreward. Calling over my shoulder, 'Hey, Mum? Mum, I reckon we should head a bit closer in.'

On shore the umbrellas and beach tents and towels and summer swimsuits. Too far away, soundless. Just the easterly in my ears. And the shadow rounding behind Mum, all three metres of it, and her getting wobbly. Me, frozen; 32 and suddenly a child again. Not turning back, or paddling out to her. Just calling over my shoulder. A voice I barely knew. Impatient. Almost peevish.

'Mum? Come on.'

And then the shadow turning away, turning north, and swimming off. To do what shadows do. Scare people. And perhaps teach them things. About how small they really are. How they are not in control. How that might be okay.

And Mum looking at me, on her new stand-up paddleboard. Trembling, but a smile already on her face, eyebrows up – the Mr Bean face she pulls when she's teasing me.

So, Santa, this Christmas, if you wish, please send me another shadow, if you like.

Warm regards,

Sam

Sam Carmody: award-winning songwriter and novelist

Dear Santa

Somewhere in my childhood you became inextricably woven with *A Christmas Carol*'s ghosts of Christmas Past, Present and Future (yes, all of them; I was raised Catholic so we're used to bizarre overlapping identities). Hence the thought of just one list or, worse still, just one wish to only one Santa, is more than a tad perplexing.

There's the World Peace wish, which seems further away each year ... so I'd appeal to the Santa trinity for that one ... because, really, what else is there?

Though if there's the possibility of adding in a few sub-wishes – in no particular order – and open to whichever Santa said wishes most appeal to, here they are:

- Everlasting collagen
- The implementation of a universal basic income
- A toaster that toasts both sides
- The irate jogger to stop yelling at my dog
- My dog to stop terrorising the irate jogger

- A very good crystal martini glass that magically appears filled with a very good and very dry vodka martini with a twist at 6 pm every Friday, which may be served by a debonair butler with white gloves, but that would be just an added bonus
- A Christmas tree that's live, that I don't kill before its time and that doesn't shed
- My father to visit his own family
- The ability to master poached eggs
- A more intimate relationship with my core abs
- Back to the debonair butler ... if they didn't mind, perhaps they could also serve me a freshly squeezed orange juice each morning – only if it's not too much trouble ... also, it would be preferable to use the oranges from my own tree ... and to do this I'd need a house with a garden where the orange tree grows ... there just happens to be a very nice one in the Byron Bay hinterland that might well do the trick
- A Christmas without regret
- Health, happiness, true love and prosperity for all

Merry Christmas and ... thanks, Santas.

JD

JD Barrett: author, scriptwriter, dreamer

Dear Santa and Mrs Claus

My Christmas wish is for a violence-free Australia. I want to wake up at Christmas without another family tragedy on the front page. I want us to create a society in which we champion respectful and equal relationships between men and women, boys and girls, and one in which violence is a thing of the past. I know this is achievable; violence is not intrinsic to the human condition.

We all have a role to play in challenging rigid gender stereotypes as well as attitudes and behaviours that may give rise to this violence in the first place. We can all be bold in speaking out against sexism, gender inequality and violence. As parents, we can model behaviours that promote gender equality and not treat our sons and daughters differently based on their sex. In some ways, it seems simple: treat others as you wish others to treat you.

And, I know this is on my list every year, but all my Christmases would come at once if we achieved equal representation of men and women, and saw our diversity and differences reflected and represented in our most powerful institutions, such as the Federal Parliament.

We can't be what we can't see! Hey, my young daughter Cordelia was surprised when Kevin Rudd became prime minister for the second time – replacing then prime minister Julia Gillard – because she didn't know that boys could be prime ministers!

So while I'm adding to my list, diverse and constructive role models would be welcome too.

I wish you both – and everyone – a peaceful and respectful Christmas.

Natasha

Natasha Stott Despoja AM: Chair, Our Watch; former leader of the Australian Democrats

Dear Santa

Please could you bring back something from the decades of a full house in the 'silly season', where I cooked for days on end from Nana's curly recipe book, cleaned up the kitchen until the early hours and the sounds of children's laughter filled the days from dawn to dusk.

I truly miss the chaos of last-minute preparations with a festive glass in hand, blending the once-a-year pav for ages and toasting the songs of Christmas with Luther Vandross, Ella Fitzgerald, Bing, Frank and Elvis, Chuck Berry, the Beach Boys and Darlene Love (not to mention the *Christmas with Col Joye* album and Chipmunks for the kids), on repeat and lifting our spirits up so high.

I even miss the pain of walking on more than the usual number of hidden Lego parts in the carpet, and cleaning up tinsel until at least Easter! And wondering if it would be wise to celebrate outdoors in the unpredictable cyclone season, or eat inside when the house was still feeling the heat from all that cooking.

Now it's much more a 'Silent Night' with the seasonal transition south of family and friends, and no matter how loud I turn up the music, it's just not the same.

Thanks, Santa, it would mean a lot to be the noisiest house in the street again. Please find anyone who can sing and needs to be fed on Christmas Day and send them here.

No grumpy men, though. Been there done that!

Sooz

Sue Camilleri: internationally adored band publicist, Chief Scout at The Stick

Acknowledgements

Santa, I couldn't have done this without you. But I kind of did. I didn't seek permission to exploit your brand and likeness. I did it anyway. Please forgive me and ask your lawyers to back off.

I reluctantly dedicate this acknowledgement to Dez Stallard. He expects a dedication, and I acknowledge that. This whole Dear Santa idea was his. I acknowledge that. Apparently all I did was email a few famous peeps. Moving on.

I'm marked as editor on the cover. I didn't edit this. I didn't have the time. And I'm not an editor. So credit where cred is due … not on the cover, but here in the acknowledgements which hopefully no one reads. Jacquie Brown was the editor. Apparently. Unofficially. Sssh. Sue Camilleri, Michala Banas and Jacinta Waters from Creative Representation sourced many of these letters. I owe you forever. Until tomorrow.

To all of our contributors, thank you for your time, for your brainwords, and for donating your letters free of charge. Maybe you're not all up yourself after all. To Chris Maddigan, for her forensic stalking skills. To Hilde Hinton, for your editorial wizardry (cough). To Shaun Tan, for that thing on the cover that wasn't good enough for his own book. To Vanessa Radnidge, for trying her best. To Lucy Freeman, to stop her banging on.

That'll do.

THE STICK

FOR PEOPLE WHO GIVE A FUCK!

Australia's kinkiest writers

Australia's most marvellous minds

Australia's plumpest ideas

For Australia's genuine readers

From the lab that produced
Dear Santa ...

thestick.org.au